ALL THE FEELINGS UNDER THE SUN

HOW TO DEAL WITH CLIMATE CHANGE

by Leslie Davenport
illustrated by Jessica Smith

Magination Press – Washington, DC – American Psychological Association

For Fiona, Will, and all the children brightening our world.
And for those yet to join us in this beautiful place—LD

Thank you to Magination Press and the American Psychological Association
for giving me the opportunity to illustrate a book that is so important
for everyone to learn a little more about right now!—JS

Books for Kids From the
American Psychological Association

Book design by Rachel Ross and Circle Graphics
Cover printed by Phoenix Color, Hagerstown, MD
Interior printed by Sheridan Books, Inc., Chelsea, MI

Library of Congress Cataloging-in-Publication Data
Names: Davenport, Leslie, author. |
Smith, Jessica (Illustrator) illustrator.
Title: All the feelings under the sun : how to deal with climate change /
by Leslie Davenport ; illustrated by Jessica Smith.
Description: Washington : Magination Press, 2021. | Includes
bibliographical references. | Summary: "A timely, thoughtful workbook
that will help young readers work through their feelings of anxiety
about climate change"— Provided by publisher.
Identifiers: LCCN 2021001043 (print) | LCCN 2021001044 (ebook) |
ISBN 9781433833915 (hardcover) | ISBN 9781433837500 (ebook)
Subjects: LCSH: Climatic changes—Juvenile literature. |
Emotions—Juvenile literature.
Classification: LCC BF353.5.C55 D38 2021 (print) | LCC BF353.5.C55 (ebook) |
DDC 155.9/15—dc23
LC record available at https://lccn.loc.gov/2021001043
LC ebook record available at https://lccn.loc.gov/2021001044

Manufactured in the United States of America
10 9 8 7 6 5 4 3 2 1

TABLE OF CONTENTS

INTRODUCTION

Climate change isn't just changing the **climate**: It's affecting every part of our world. To help you understand the transformation of our planet that's happening right now, this book will take you on a journey through many different branches of science, our history, our societies and cultures, and into your own mind and feelings. As you learn about **climate change**, you'll also be learning about yourself.

You'll discover all the ways that nature is beautiful, powerful, delicate, fierce, mysterious, and awesome. But nature isn't just outside of us in the trees, fish, clouds, and lakes: We humans are a part of nature. We share the same history and we're made from the same elements as everything else on the planet, like hydrogen, oxygen, and phosphorus. We live in and share the **biosphere**. We each have a place in our planet's living system with all of the world's plants and its other animals, from the sky to the earth to the sea.

This book will look back to the origins of the Earth and the evolution of life up to the present day. We'll learn about the different scientific predictions for our future, which depend on how successfully we humans can deal with climate change. You'll learn how climate change started, why it's creating problems, and all the ways you can respond to its challenges.

You'll be introduced to some of the many people who are devoting their time and energy to finding climate solutions that will contribute to a safer and healthier world for everyone. You'll see how solutions from different fields—like farming, transportation, clean energy production, and the restoration and protection of land, water, and air—can join together to create a new and healthier world. Since we all contribute to the life force of the planet, you'll discover many things you do that can make a difference, and you'll find strength in learning about and making these choices. You might be inspired by the creative ideas you'll read about and the accomplishments of the many youth leaders in the climate movement.

A very important part of our journey into our own and our planet's future is learning how to build our inner resiliency: our emotional strength. It's a remarkable time to be alive, because we'll all be working together to deal with the huge challenges to our planet. As we learn more about the impacts of climate change, at times it may be frightening or sad and make us nervous or angry or more. You may experience all the feelings under the sun. These feelings are totally natural and healthy. You'll be learning more about what you're feeling and why, and this book will give you some new tools to express your feelings so they don't overwhelm you. In fact, strong feelings can be helpful: They can give you the energy and focus you need to nourish your dreams and act in creative and productive ways.

This book is meant to be read slowly, and you'll find exercises in each chapter that explore how the feelings and ideas you read about fit into your own life. Take your time. Most of the activities use writing or drawing, so if you want, you can make a "Making a Healthier World Together" journal to use as you read this book. You can use a blank book and decorate it, or simply use sheets of paper.

Feelings and Climate Change

Paying close attention to our feelings will give us useful information about our life experiences and even help us move toward climate change solutions. For example, anger can help you take a stand in the world to protect who you are and what you feel and believe. But just like natural **ecosystems**, we need a healthy balance. Too much anger, and you risk hurting others—but if you don't acknowledge the natural anger that you feel in a situation, you risk giving up your valuable point of view and your individuality.

Fear is a feeling that lets us know that change is happening. It can help us take care of ourselves and avoid harm or injury. Too much fear, though, can prevent us from doing things that we might enjoy or need to do—and too little fear could put us in dangerous situations.

Feeling sadness can sometimes help us see that we need to let go of something: Maybe there's a situation that no longer works for us, and it's time to make room for something new. Or we've lost something we love, like our pet. But feeling sad all the time might make it hard to concentrate in school or hang out with friends.

A Pause for Feelings

Take five minutes and write in your journal or on a sheet of paper about some times you felt anger, fear, and sadness. As you remember those feelings, write about how they made sense with what was happening at the time.

Feelings are like the **weather**: They come and go, and they're always changing. There are days full of fun that feel like a bright sunny day, and on other days our feelings are dark and stormy. We often only pay attention to the big feelings: being mad, scared, excited, or sad. But there are subtle feelings too: feeling calm, a little nervous, relieved, bored, or silly. The more you pay attention to all your feelings, name them, and learn how to express them, the more they'll flow and change like the weather. They'll help you understand yourself and move confidently through your life.

YOUR INTERNAL WEATHER REPORT

In a journal or on a separate sheet of paper, describe your feelings in this moment like you're giving a weather report. You can use some of the terms from the list below or come up with your own:

Sunny with a few clouds

Chance of rain

Hazy

Stormy

Chance of snow

Blustery wind

Clear skies

Unpredictable weather

Warm and breezy

Describe your internal weather three times a day for one week to see if there's a weather pattern. You can use the following chart as a model or create your own design.

YOUR INTERNAL WEATHER REPORT

MORNING:

AFTERNOON:

EVENING:

Global Warming, Climate Change, and Weather

In this book, you'll learn many terms that will be helpful for understanding climate change. Some of these ideas come from science, and others come from psychology to describe the feelings that are part of facing a world that's heating up. It's important that the facts and the feelings move forward hand in hand, so that we find ways to feel strong as we discover how to create a healthier world. Let's start by defining some of the basic scientific terms and sort out the difference between global warming, climate change, and weather.

Global warming is the term used to describe the increasing temperature of the Earth's surface, including the oceans. Some climate scientists like the term "global weirding" to describe the hot and cold weather-related extremes you'll be learning more about.

Climate change refers to all the ways these rising temperatures are affecting plants, animals, people, and the environment. Because changes are happening so quickly, many scientists are sounding the alarm, and refer to our current times as a climate crisis.

It's easy to confuse climate and weather. *Weather* describes what's happening over the next few hours, days, or weeks. For example, you might say, "The weather has been hot and humid this week." The weather might start out sunny and warm, and then there are several rainy, foggy days in a row. *Climate*, on the other hand, describes big patterns in the weather over a long period of time in a particular place (or the whole planet itself): It's usually measured in spans of 30 years or more. If you're thinking about moving to a new place, you'll probably want to find out what kind of climate it has. Do you want to live in a tropical, arctic, or dry desert climate? The difference between weather and climate explains how we can still have cool-weather days even though the overall climate is warming.

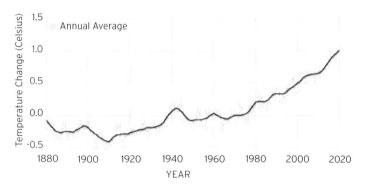

Data courtesy of NASA

Scientists began recording the temperature in various parts of the world in 1851, so they have more than 160 years of weather information that is helping them see the big changes in the climate and the overall direction of the planet's temperature. Since record keeping began, two-thirds of the warming has happened since 1975! Climate scientists began to notice that every year was breaking records for the hottest year ever recorded in many parts of the world. And this warming trend will continue if we humans don't make changes.

But it's not just the warming temperatures that tell us that climate change is happening. Scientists are like detectives searching for clues and putting the pieces of a puzzle together. They study all the parts of our ecosystems, including forests, fossils, ice, deserts, coral reefs, the atmosphere, tree rings, mud, ocean water, plants, the tropics, and insects to learn about the many changes that are happening. What they've discovered is that the impact of climate change can be seen all over the world. In this book we'll be learning about many of those impacts. While it can be scary and sad to learn about them, we'll also talk about ways to build emotional strength to face these challenges so that it's easier to be part of the solution.

Here are a few examples of what scientists have learned:

- Air pollution is a global public health emergency, killing 250,000 Americans every year, and more than 3 million in China and India combined.

- Glacier National Park used to have 150 glaciers, but today there are only 26.

- Since we began record-keeping in 1851, the sea level has risen about eight inches across the planet as a result of melting ice. Because the Earth is continuing to warm, scientists predict that the sea level could rise another six feet by 2100. This will be catastrophic for people and animals who live on the coasts or on islands.

- ◐ Climate change is also making our weather more extreme and unpredictable. In the last 50 years, scientists have measured more and more intense storms like hurricanes and floods from heavier than usual rainfall.

- ◐ Because the oceans absorb much of the extra heat and carbon dioxide from our warming atmosphere, the water has become about 30% more acidic.

You'll learn more about ecosystems—how all the world's plants and animals live together in a balanced relationship with their environment. But you'll also see how changes like increased acid in the oceans have far-reaching consequences, like the destruction of coral reefs, the overall ocean food chain, and the health of all ocean life.

But our concerns about climate change aren't limited to plants, animals, air, and the water. As animals, we humans are part of the Earth's living ecosystems, and we need all of our planet's elements to be in a healthy balance. People who rely on ocean and coastal resources to make a living are already being affected. This is happening in parts of the Gulf Coast of the United States— Texas, Louisiana, Mississippi, Alabama, and Florida— and also on the west coast and Alaska. In the Puget

Sound area of the Pacific Northwest of the United States, the salmon population is declining, and that's threatening the Suquamish Native American tribe's nutritional and economic system and even their cultural heritage. You'll read about many examples like this as we look at the global effects of climate change.

Learning about climate change can be upsetting, and it's natural and even healthy to feel alarmed at times: These feelings are a signal that something's wrong and needs our attention. It doesn't mean that you should go through your day being upset, but it does mean that if these feelings occur, you're paying attention to what's important in our world. It's important to take care of yourself so you don't feel too burdened by what you've learned.

BUTTERFLY HUG

What are you feeling after reading about some of the ways our world is changing? There may be more than one feeling. In your journal or on a piece of paper, write down the feelings that are the strongest. Assign how strong each feeling is using a number 0–10, where 0 is not upset at all, 5 is kind of upset, and 10 is very upset.

The "butterfly hug" is a simple activity you can do to help calm yourself when you're feeling upset. You can sit or stand, whichever you choose.

1. Cross your arms over your chest with the tips of your fingers pointing up toward the sky, letting them rest where you can feel your collarbones, those firm, bony bridges across the top of your chest just below your shoulders.

2. Now hook your thumbs together to form the body of the butterfly, and your hands and fingers will be its wings. Your eyes can be closed, or partly closed looking down toward the ground.

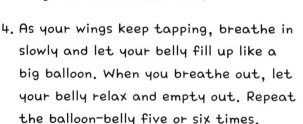

3. Begin to lift each wing one at a time while the butterfly body rests on your chest. Feel the tips of the wings tapping against your collarbones, right, left, right, left. Keep going, letting the wings be relaxed and free.

4. As your wings keep tapping, breathe in slowly and let your belly fill up like a big balloon. When you breathe out, let your belly relax and empty out. Repeat the balloon-belly five or six times.

5. Keep your soft butterfly wings gently tap, tap, tapping, right, left, right, left. Let yourself remember a place where you feel relaxed and safe. Maybe it's outdoors, maybe it's your own room or you can imagine a place you'd like to go that has all your favorite things. As you imagine yourself in your own special, safe place, look around. Are there flowers and blue skies, or is it a cozy spot to curl up with your pet? It can have other people, or it can be just for you. You can run and play and make lots of noise, or quietly rest.

6. Keep your butterfly wings tapping while you explore and enjoy this place for about five minutes. Then let your butterfly rest, letting your arms come down by your sides, and open your eyes.

7. Now rate your feelings again, on the same 0–10 scale. Have they changed?

8. Take out your journal or a sheet of paper and draw your safe and special place.

You can do this activity any time you feel worried or upset, or just want to relax.

About This Book

Reading this book will give you a full picture of the challenges of climate change and the many different ways to be involved, and it will teach you exercises to help you build courage and strength for helping to create a cleaner, safer world. In order to actually build your emotional strength, it's important to take the time to work through the practices that are included in each chapter.

Here's what you'll be discovering in this book: Chapter 1, "How We Know What We Know," will give you an overview of the evolution of our planet and life on Earth, and it will describe how the **Industrial Revolution** set us on the path toward climate change. You'll also learn practices that will help you connect with some of the remarkable and surprising aspects of the natural world.

Chapter 2, "The Earth is Heating Up," will give you a deeper look at why just several degrees of warming can have such a big impact, and you'll read about people already being forced to move their communities because of rising seas. It's painful to learn about the harm and losses that people, places, and animals are experiencing, and you'll learn to work with the fear and **eco-grief** that comes from being a kind and caring person.

In Chapter 3, "Everything is Connected," you'll discover that decisions guided by an understanding of our interconnectedness is one of the keys to helping the world heal. It can be upsetting to recognize how far we have to go to create a society that's built on Earth-wise values. We'll continue to look at these natural feelings and explore, express, and support them.

In Chapter 4, "Practicing Eco-Justice," you'll learn what eco-justice and climate justice mean, and how they bring human rights into our study of climate change. You'll complete a personal values inventory so that your own beliefs about what's right and fair can guide your actions more and more, and you'll work on activities that build up your ability to tolerate your biggest feelings.

Chapter 5, "Making a Healthier World Together," will show you that, while there's still a lot of work to be done to heal our biosphere, there's exciting progress happening all around the planet Earth where life can be found, from high in the sky to the bottom of the ocean. You'll be guided to find your own unique ways to bring your interests, talents, and passion into actions that support a healthier environment.

A lot of kids and young adults are interested in climate change. You've probably heard about Greta Thunberg, but there's also Jaden Anthony, Levi Draheim, Autumn Peltier, Lilly Platt, youth groups like the Zero Hour and Sunrise Movement, and many more. You might be surprised to see that climate activists don't always carry signs out in the street:

There are lots of ways that youth leaders are making a difference with art, writing, legal efforts, and social media campaigns, just to name a few. Diversity is important in all areas of life, but especially when it comes to transforming our world, which will happen faster if each one of us brings forward our unique viewpoints and strengths. Every chapter in this book will profile a youth leader who's making a difference in building a healthier, safer world. Maybe they're a lot like you.

So let's begin this important journey equipped with a few essential supplies: curiosity, an open mind, and a growing toolkit of practices that will boost your self-care and fuel your positive emotional energy. We'll be picking up additional resources along the way from science, psychology, and Earth-wise traditions as we creatively confront the vital topic of healing our warming planet.

Greta Thunberg

Greta was born in Stockholm, Sweden, and began learning about climate change at the age of eight. She became so sad and confused that she stopped eating and talking for a while. Why wasn't more being done to make things better? Since then, she's taken a stand and reclaimed her voice in a very powerful way.

When Greta was 15, she was inspired by teenage activists in Florida who were protesting gun violence. The Civil Rights activist Rosa Parks was also a role model for her decision to take action. Greta decided to try something like Parks did, and so instead of going to school she sat outside the Swedish Parliament building alone with a homemade sign that read "School Strike for Climate." She wanted politicians to take notice and create clean energy laws.

The newspapers began telling her story, and when she was just 16 so many people were inspired by her action that the first Global Strike for Climate in March 2019 drew over 1.6 million people from 125 countries. Since then, Greta has given many speeches that challenge the world's leaders in places like the European Union Parliament and the United Nations Climate Action Summit in New York City. She's the youngest person ever to be named *Time* magazine's "Person of the Year," and she was even nominated to receive the Nobel Peace Prize. Greta is a powerful influence who's helping many people find the courage to stand up and demand that we meet the urgent needs of our planet.

Greta wasn't looking for fame, she was simply following her passionate feelings about making a difference. What passionate feelings do you have? Are they inspiring you to take action? Her actions can encourage all of us to find our own ways to do the same.

chapter 1:

HOW WE KNOW WHAT WE KNOW

I f you live in a place where not much has changed, it might be hard to imagine the rising sea level and gigantic storms happening around our warming planet. Maybe there haven't been many interruptions to your enjoyment of your food, friends, and comfortable home. But if you've ever had to outrun a flood, fire, or hurricane, or you know someone who has, it's easier to understand all the concerns about climate change. Unfortunately, no place on the planet is free from the challenges of climate change; it's just that some places are experiencing them first, or more intensely.

UNDERSTANDING OUR WORLD THROUGH SCIENCE

When it comes to climate change, we need to look beyond our personal experience and study information that comes to us through science. Consider these simple but amazing facts that would be hard to believe without their proof by scientific tools:

- We live on a planet that's basically a mud-ball hurtling through space at 67,000 miles per hour. That's 10,000 times faster than cars drive on the freeway! That can certainly be strange to hear, because we all feel like we're standing still.

◐ When we look into the night sky, we can enjoy the beauty of the stars and the moon. Astronomers who study the sky say there are 21,600,000,000,000,000,000,000,000 other planets in our expanding universe— and they're still counting!

◐ There is dust from ancient stars in our bodies. When you stretch your muscles or look at your hands, it can be hard to believe that there's stardust contained there too.

We enjoy our natural environment through our senses: the smell of pine needles, the sweetness of a peach, the feeling of cool, silky water when we swim, the colors of a sunset, the sound of gentle rain. When we add scientific knowledge that goes beyond what our senses and direct observations can tell us, even a small, simple thing can open up worlds of mystery.

Maybe you've seen bluebell flowers growing in a garden, or a picture of one in a book. The flower has delicate purple and blue bell-shaped petals. Did you know that juice from that plant can be used for glue, to treat snakebites, and even as part of laundry soap? It's amazing that this small blue flower is more than just beautiful: It's useful! You've probably walked right by plants that are used to make some of the medicines we rely on: Yew trees are used to make a strong chemotherapy medication for treating cancer; foxglove is made into a lifesaving drug that strengthens the heart; swelling and inflammation can be reduced with horse chestnut. But we need science to help us discover the right medicinal use; it can be dangerous to eat these plants without understanding their properties! Many plants and natural elements are life-giving, and part of reversing climate change is increasing our awareness and appreciation of our close relationship with the natural world.

Scientists use many different kinds of technical devices that analyze our natural environment and can help make sense of climate change. These devises can measure things like the nutrient properties of soil, underground water patterns, the origins of life in space, and even the history of our world in mile-deep ice samples from Antarctica. The scientific approach will take the lead as we're learning about climate change. But we'll also study other ways of understanding our planet, including cultural traditions that have proven their value for thousands of years.

I Am Nature

Take a moment to really consider and feel that you *are* nature, sharing your personal history with the trees and stars, and sharing **DNA**—life's basic building blocks—with pets, wild animals, and all people. Some kids say it feels like there is a warmth in their chest that spreads through their body. Others begin to notice a stronger feeling of the earth under their feet. If this it a new idea, it might feel odd. It might even make your head hurt as your mind expands to think about things in a new way. What does it feel like in your body right now as you view yourself as a part of nature?

In Chapter 3, you'll be reading more about what we can learn from **Indigenous** traditions about seeing all parts of nature as our "relatives." For now, draw a picture that illustrates this new way of thinking: include yourself in the picture along with your connection to the sun, moon, and oceans, and your rooted, furry, or finned family.

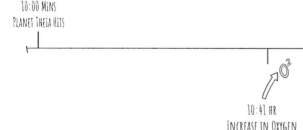

10:00 Mins
Planet Theia Hits

10:41 hr
Increase in Oxygen

A Super-Quick History of the Planet

Scientists tell us that our universe began with a Big Bang 13 billion years ago. Planet Earth formed just 4.5 billion years ago. It took millions of years after that for life like plants and then animals to emerge. Check out the bottom of these pages for a timeline of some important events . . . if the 4.5 billion-year history of the Earth were condensed into 24 hours! When we look at the timeline, we humans are brand-new! That's why we're still figuring out how to live properly on the Earth. We're very intelligent and we've invented lots of amazing things, but we make mistakes, and part of responding to climate change is figuring out how to fix our mistakes and live in a more balanced relationship with all the other life on Earth.

The Earth has taken many different forms in the millions of years before life evolved. At the very beginning, it was a fireball. Later it looked like a snowball flying through space, completely covered in snow and ice. Because of the fossils that scientists find, we know

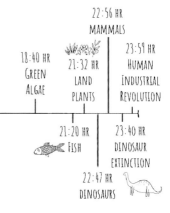

22:56 HR
MAMMALS

18:40 HR
GREEN
ALGAE

21:32 HR
LAND
PLANTS

23:59 HR
HUMAN
INDUSTRIAL
REVOLUTION

21:20 HR
FISH

23:40 HR
DINOSAUR
EXTINCTION

22:47 HR
DINOSAURS

there was a time when dinosaurs roamed the Earth—for 165 million years! The planet has always been changing, and it's changing now too . . . but for very different reasons.

How Climate Change Began

Once humans had been here for a while, we began to figure out how to use metals like steel and copper to make tools and eventually machines. Then we learned how to use coal as a fuel and how to generate electricity. Around the time that your great-great-great-great-great-great-great grandparents lived was the era known as the Industrial Revolution. From about 1760 to 1840, people invented many fantastic things. Instead of going places by walking or riding a horse, we built engines that powered the first cars and trains. It used to take four days to walk to another town, but now you could hop on a train and be there in just four hours. We created factories with machines that could quickly weave cloth instead of making it by hand on a loom. We invented

the first lightbulb to replace candlelight. There was a feeling of excitement in the air: Everything was now bigger, faster, easier, and better. Or so it seemed.

For the next 200 years we created even more modern conveniences: concrete highways, plastics, chemicals that make food grow faster, huge ships that carry products between countries, bigger factories, nuclear power plants, and airplanes. It wasn't until the mid-1900s that we discovered a major problem with these inventions: They are all powered by fuels that produce carbon emissions, the main culprit in heating up the planet.

The Industrial Revolution and Colonization

The Industrial Revolution created an additional problem. To get the raw materials and labor needed for quickly building trains, planes, and other inventions, there was (and continues to be) widespread exploitation of many lands and peoples. Forcibly exerting control over natural

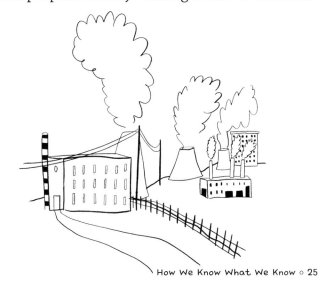

resources, and then making the same people and places dependent on the new society (such as taking and then charging for water or land that used to be freely available) is called **colonization**. While the origins of colonization are much older than the Industrial Revolution, this push for rapid progress ingrained a colonial mindset even further into people's everyday lives. Especially for Indigenous communities, there have been devastating land-grabs and a disruption of cultural identities. You will be learning more about restoring these kinds of human rights abuses when you read about eco-justice in Chapter 4.

Balloon Breathing

One of the very best tools for calming yourself down when you feel upset or overwhelmed is available to you anytime, anywhere, free of charge: mindful breathing. There are many techniques for breathing in specific ways that help calm your body, mind, and emotions. In this exercise you can give "balloon breathing" a try following the steps below.

1. On a sheet of paper or in your journal, write down a number on a scale from 0–10 that describes how you're feeling right now, with 0 being no distress and 10 being very upset.

2. Sit or stand in a comfortable position: Your eyes can be open or closed, whichever is more relaxing for you.

3. Place your hands about six inches in front of your face, palms facing each other, like you're holding a small balloon between them.

4. Breathe in slowly and fully through your nose for four counts, hands staying where they are. Pick a breathing speed that's comfortable for you.

5. Breathe out through your mouth for six counts while slowly spreading your hands farther apart, like you're slowly blowing up the balloon with your breath.

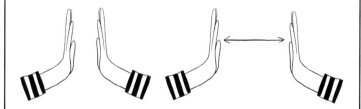

6. Then, slowly move your hands together as you breath in for a count of four, as if you're sucking all the air back out of the balloon. Repeat this out and in cycle three times.

7. After doing the balloon breathing three times, pause and let your breath find its own natural rhythm and pace without controlling it. You can rest your arms at your sides.

8. Notice how you feel, and write another number between 0-10 in your journal or on your paper that indicates how calm or stressed you feel right now. You can write any other things you notice or feel after doing the balloon breath, too.

OUR CARBON FOOTPRINT

Your footprint in the sand or snow shows that you've been there. Every time we burn fossil fuels—oil, coal, and natural gas—they release carbon dioxide (also known by its chemical name, **CO_2**) into the atmosphere. The amount of CO_2 released by a specific activity is called its **carbon footprint**. Cooking an egg on the stove leaves a relatively small footprint; flying across the country to visit relatives leaves a big one because of the large amount of CO_2 that airplanes emit by burning jet fuel.

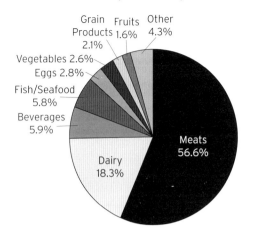

Carbon Footprint by Food Group

- Grain Products 2.1%
- Fruits 1.6%
- Other 4.3%
- Vegetables 2.6%
- Eggs 2.8%
- Fish/Seafood 5.8%
- Beverages 5.9%
- Dairy 18.3%
- Meats 56.6%

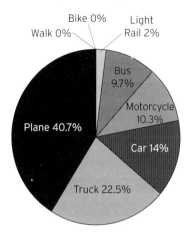

Carbon Footprint per Passenger in Transportation

- Walk 0%
- Bike 0%
- Light Rail 2%
- Bus 9.7%
- Motorcycle 10.3%
- Car 14%
- Truck 22.5%
- Plane 40.7%

This brings us to the main challenge of climate change. Not only do we enjoy our cars, clothes, electric lights, fast foods, and all our other conveniences, but we've built our society to totally rely on them. People's everyday lives are completely woven together with the fossil-fuel burning, carbon-emitting systems. It's easy to forget that nearly every product we buy and use has some carbon emission as part of its manufacturing. When we take a car or plane ride, we're usually not thinking about how the fuel that's being burned was extracted from deep underground by big machines (which themselves run on fuel) and transported long distances to where we're using it (by trains or trucks that also burn fuel). A big part of becoming eco-wise is reminding ourselves of the real cost—the cost to the planet and everything on it—of what we're doing and how we're doing it in our everyday lives.

Since the start of the Industrial Revolution, large amounts of CO_2 and other damaging **greenhouse gases** like methane have been pumped into the atmosphere by the factories and technologies that give us our modern way of life. Climate scientists agree that transitioning to a world no longer reliant on fossil fuels by using renewable energy sources like wind and solar needs to happen as soon as possible. The Industrial Revolution was an exciting time overflowing with creativity, but now we need a whole new kind of creativity and new discoveries to find ways of living that don't damage the Earth. We can use our growing understanding of ways we've gotten out of balance with our biosphere to guide our imaginations toward helpful change.

MIXED FEELINGS

We can have more than one feeling about a situation, and that can feel like a tug-of-war, with one idea or feeling pulling us in one direction and a different one pulling us the opposite way. For example, you might want to go to soccer practice because you really enjoy soccer, but you might also want to lay on the couch and watch TV. Both of these desires can exist in us at the same time. Recognizing and moving though our mixed feelings is one of the keys to understanding climate change and making greener choices.

1. In your journal or on a piece of paper, make a list of the numbers one through five, and after each number write the following sentence.
I need/want to _____, but I also need/want to _____.

2. Fill in the blanks with the things you're considering changing to reduce your carbon footprint. Here's an example: I want to get to school and soccer practice on time, but I also want to avoid driving because I know that cars add too much carbon to the atmosphere.

3. After you've filled in all five sentences, go back to each one and write in possible solutions.

Example: When the weather's good, I can walk with friends to school or plan to ride our bikes together. I haven't tried the school bus, but will check it out. I'll see if I can arrange a carpool so fewer cars are being used.

4. Write about how you feel when you know that you're taking action to shrink your carbon footprint.

We've put so much carbon into the atmosphere that it's formed an invisible blanket around the Earth that traps the sun's heat, causing temperatures all over the planet to rise. The trapped heat is called the "greenhouse effect." We know how nice a cozy blanket can feel, but when we get too hot, we take it off and cool down. Unfortunately, the Earth can't kick off its blanket of CO_2, and now it's heating up.

Lilly Platt

Lilly's big dream to make the world plastic-free began when she was just seven years old. On a neighborhood walk with her grandfather, Lilly began counting all the throw-away pieces of plastic she passed. She counted 91 in less than 20 minutes! Her grandfather, a geologist, told her how almost all plastic on the ground ends up in the ocean. She was so upset by the ways that plastic harms marine animals that she committed right then and there to do something about it.

She started "Lilly's Plastic Pickup" campaign: She immediately began avoiding single-use plastics whenever possible and picking up plastic trash wherever she went. One year she collected 25,000 pieces! She posted photos of her campaign on Facebook and Twitter and now has thousands of followers who are inspired to join her clean-up efforts from wherever on the planet they live.

Originally from England, Lilly now lives in the Netherlands, and she's known internationally as one of the top 100 influencers tackling plastic contamination. She's become a youth ambassador for many organizations, including the Plastic Pollution Coalition, World Cleanup Day, HOW Global, and others. While she'll always continue her efforts to create a plastic-free world, she's also expanded her involvement in climate activism and joins other youth around the world in climate strikes to influence governments to create green energy policies.

Lilly has been asked if she'd rather spend time with toy bricks or dolls, but she's always answered, "This is what I want to do! Children can make a change, and their voices need to be heard."

How do you feel? What do you want to do?

chapter 2:

THE EARTH IS HEATING UP

When you hear about three, four, or five degrees of warming in the Earth's temperature, it doesn't seem like a big deal. If the weather used to be 75 degrees and now it's going to be 80, wouldn't that make it even nicer to be outside? But the overall "global" warming that scientists describe works in a different way—it's not just about the local weather. If you've ever had a fever of 101, 102, or 103 degrees, not only is it uncomfortable, it can be dangerous—even though it's only a few degrees higher than our normal body temperature! When you have a fever that stays high, you might even need to go to the emergency room. Our biosphere is also sensitive to small temperature increases, just like our bodies. Some people are declaring that the Earth's fever is a climate emergency and that it needs urgent care.

Our bodies are themselves an ecosystem, and they work just like the larger planetary ones do: All the parts rely on each other and need to be in balance to stay healthy. Our organs can be harmed when we have a high fever that continues for a long time. The Earth's rising temperature is harming many of its inter-connected systems and inhabitants.

Eco-Grief

It's painful to learn about the damage being done to the people, communities, land, animals, and oceans that you'll be reading about in this book. We want to keep swimming in our favorite rivers and lakes; we don't want to see them become too polluted for humans, or to see all the fish die. We want to play outside with our friends without it being unbearably hot or having it hurt to breathe from smoke or air pollution. When we lose something in our environment or we experience a personal loss due to an extreme weather event (or even when we think about possible losses in the future) strong feelings naturally occur. The natural reaction to loss is grief, and when those losses come from climate change, it's called "environmental grief," or simply "eco-grief."

Grief is more than just feelings of sadness, and the different kinds of grief often change over time. These are some of the common ways that eco-grief is experienced in our thoughts and feelings:

- **Denial:** You just can't believe that what's happening to people, places, and animals due to climate change is true. Maybe the reports are wrong or they're exaggerated. It's hard to imagine the struggles that are happening in other parts of the world. You'd rather put it out of your mind and focus on just about anything else.

- **Anger:** You're mad that climate change is happening and that adults haven't done more to repair their mistakes. It's not fair that this is something that you, a kid, have to deal with. It's just not right, and you're angry.

- **Bargaining:** You'd like a fast, easy way to feel better about climate change. You try to figure out a way to quickly reduce the danger and damage from climate change: Maybe everything will be okay if you just stop using plastic straws?

- **Depression:** You feel really sad because you understand that the changes and the threats to the Earth are real. You wish you could ease the suffering of others,

and it breaks your heart to imagine
the hardships that people and animals
are facing. You also may feel helpless
to do anything about it. You might
not feel like hanging out with your
friends or participating in your usual
activities much anymore. Your heart
can feel heavy, and there may be
tearful times.

◐ Acceptance: You realize that while
climate change has created big
challenges, your life is bigger than this
single topic. There are many times of
fun and of loving connections with people,
and there are beautiful places in nature
or in cities to enjoy. You realize that
you can help with the solutions because
each one of us is part of the Earth's
life force, and you don't have to face
this alone. You're part of a larger
movement of many people who are
committed to making a healthier
world for all beings.

Sometimes it's our bodies rather than our thoughts
or feelings that express our grief. Grief can cause a
stomachache, make you extra tired, keep you awake at
night, or you might feel like there's a rock in your heart
or a tight band in your throat. Even normal noises can
seem louder and more irritating than they used to.

It's important to learn how eco-grief communic
to you so you can respond in a kind and loving way
toward yourself.

ECO-GRIEF NOTES

As you read about the impacts of climate change,
keep your climate change journal or a piece of
paper nearby and write down your thoughts
and feelings that match the descriptions of grief
you've just read about. There might be others,
too. You've learned that like the weather, your
feelings change. They come and they go. And
one of the best ways to keep them flowing is
to recognize them, let them have their say, and
express them.

There's no right or wrong way to grieve, and
there's no set timeline. You might notice that you
experience several kinds of grief, or that your
feelings bounce from one to another, or that you
experience more than one at a time. For example,
you might have accepted that climate change is
happening, and maybe you're involved in efforts
to improve our situation, but you still feel sad.
You might not be grieving right now, but if those
feelings come up later, you can come back to
this activity.

How Climate Change Is Affecting Wildlife and People

When people, plants and animals have lived in a particular part of the world for a long time, they learn to thrive in their environment. For example, polar bears have gradually evolved to enjoy their home on cold ice sheets, because their thick layers of fat and fur keep them warm. Beluga whales, snowy owls, and Canadian lynx are some of the other animals that have developed so they can live successfully in icy Arctic regions. Now that the Earth is warming, though, much of the snow and ice that these animals rely on is beginning to melt. Sea ice is where polar bears raise their baby cubs, and it's their place to rest after long periods of swimming to hunt for seals. Now that there's much less sea ice, these bears have to work extra hard to swim longer distances for food, which leaves them exhausted and starving. Unless we make big changes and turn climate change around, scientists predict the polar bear population

could disappear by the middle of this century. That's just 30 years from now.

The carbon blanket that's heating the Earth is creating problems like this all over the world. Every day, each elephant that lives in Africa needs to drink about as much water as a bathtub holds. Because the climate is warmer there now though, it doesn't rain as much in certain parts of Africa, and elephants now need to walk longer distances to search for fresh water. As you can imagine, this is hard for baby elephant calves and older

elephants. Koala bears are nearly extinct in Australia because of the enormous increase in wildfires there, and also because the growing amount of CO_2 in the air is killing their main food source, eucalyptus leaves. When a place gets much less rainfall than it used to, it's called a drought, and climate change is dramatically increasing periods of drought in many parts of the world. These areas are now struggling to get enough water for plants, animals, and people to stay alive. The state of California is one of many places that's having periods of severe drought, and its record-breaking heat waves have dried out the trees and grass and made wildfires a year-round threat to homes, communities, plants, and animals.

When we think about our warming climate, it makes sense that ice would melt and dry areas would get drier: but what about the flooding, the "mega hurricanes," and the extreme snowstorms that scientists say are also caused by climate change? In addition to the overall warming trend, climate change is creating "weather chaos": unpredictable weather patterns caused by how the warming atmosphere is changing the position of the **jet streams**.

The Changing Jet Streams

High in the atmosphere (five to nine miles above the ground!) there are four bands of wind and gases called the "jet streams." They flow in fast-moving currents at 120 to 250 miles per hour. If we could see them, they'd look a lot like rivers. There are two polar jet streams close to the north and south poles and two subtropical ones near the equator. The jet streams create barriers between masses of warmer and cooler air, and this has created and maintained stable temperatures and predictable weather and seasons for thousands of years.

Having the same seasons every year is important for keeping ecosystems of plants, animals, and communities healthy and adaptable. For example, Arctic foxes have evolved to live in a snowy, icy environment. They have fluffy white fur that camouflages them in the snow, and they're chubby to hold in their body heat. The Fennec fox that lives in hot, sandy deserts has developed large, bat-like ears that help them get rid of body heat and stay cool. In order for these two kinds of foxes to thrive, the places they live need to stay almost the same from season to season and year to year: cold and snowy, or hot and dry.

But scientists tell us that global warming is changing the jet streams. When the Arctic jet stream takes a dramatic new dip toward the south, it carries pockets of cold air with it. It also might suddenly slow down and stop so that the icy air hovers in place, keeping the weather below it frigid with cold and heavier than usual snowfalls, or torrential rain that causes destructive flooding. The equatorial jet stream is also carrying warm air farther north than it used to, and it's doing it more often. That's making the Arctic warm faster than other parts of the Earth, melting glaciers and ice sheets that have been frozen for thousands of years, and making the sea level rise all over the world.

How do scientists know that climate change is what made the jet streams change their movements and lead to more dramatic seasonal and weather events? One way that scientists study these changes is indirectly, by looking at the patterns in tree rings (the different-colored circles inside the trunks of trees). When there's a wide, even ring in the trunk, biologists know that the tree had a healthy growing season that year with plenty of rain and sunshine. During a year of drought, the tree barely grows, and it creates little or no ring. Beginning in 1960, tree rings around the world began showing new patterns that matched more extreme weather events. Such big shifts had never been seen in the 290 years that scientists had been studying them. The tree rings are like a map that matches up perfectly with the beginning of the increase in extreme weather events all over the planet, including thinner rings during heat waves, droughts, and wildfires, and wider rings in times of flooding. By this time, the industrial revolution was in full swing and the atmospheric CO_2 levels were significantly increasing. When atmospheric chemists and physicists added their information about changes in the Earth's temperature, air pressure, and water vapor patterns, it all pointed to the same conclusion: The warming atmosphere caused the movement of the jet streams to change and the climate to change with them.

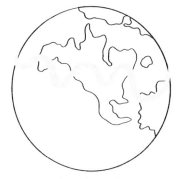

stable jet stream   wavy from climate change

Part of what makes climate change so alarming is that these big changes in the Earth's atmosphere are new, and even the most experienced scientists can't predict what the future will bring. But that's also why we can be hopeful: The uncertainty leaves room for positive change and new possibilities . . . *if* we can start doing things differently! We created these problems mainly by burning fossil fuels, and we can now choose greener energy sources like wind and solar power and create a different future.

Because it's well-known that human activities created these changes to the biosphere, it's been proposed that we name this era in the Earth's history the Anthropocene era. "Anthropo-" means "human" and "-cene" means epoch, a period of geologic time. Wouldn't it be great if this era could describe all the wonderful things that humans do, including changing the way we live to be more in harmony with the planet? This and more can be our goal.

EXTINCTIONS

The natural history of the Earth includes periods of dramatic changes that involve the death of many plants and animals in a short period of time. These are called "mass extinctions." The extinctions often involve both a loss of existing life forms and the evolution of new ones soon after. Scientists have discovered at least five periods of mass extinction, and they've been triggered by events like rare and enormous eruptions of volcanoes whose ash and smoke were so thick they blocked the sun and cooled the climate. Once, a huge asteroid hit the Earth with similar effects; that's what scientists currently believe caused the extinction of the dinosaurs. Changes in biodiversity—the variety and interdependence of all the living things in a particular place, or on the entire planet—are a normal occurrence, but scientists now believe that climate change is speeding up the rate of extinction so that it's somewhere between ten to hundreds of times faster than before the Industrial Revolution. Two-thirds of our oceans and three-quarters of our land have been severely altered, making it harder for plants and animals to survive.

In 2019, 450 researchers wrote a report to the United Nations after examining 15,000 scientific and government research studies. The studies told them that one-million species of plants and animals are currently being threatened. This is a loud call to action that we can all respond to. The report pointed out several problem areas that we can focus on:

- Burning of fossil fuels, which is making it too hot, wet, or dry for some species.
- Pollution of water, land, and the food chain with toxins.
- Overgrowth of invasive species (when a plant or animal is accidentally introduced into a new ecosystem where it doesn't normally live, and starts crowding out native plants or animals).
- Overfishing of the oceans, which is killing off fish populations at a dramatic speed and upsetting the balance between many different parts of ocean ecosystems.

When you begin to see the big picture of climate change, it becomes clearer just how complex and far-reaching the consequences are. This can feel overwhelming at times, and while it's helpful to understand the full extent of the problems, we need to remember that almost all change comes from small and consistent steps. Picture for a moment a stained-glass window made of many colorful pieces of glass that together create a beautiful picture. We enjoy the beauty of the overall design, but to create it, the artisans had to measure and cut each piece, one at a time. It didn't look like much when there were just were pieces of glass sitting in a box, or it was just an idea in the artist's mind. It took patience, persistence, skill, creativity, and vision. These same qualities can guide the programs and actions we'll all be doing together to build a safer world. Let's work with some of the colorful pieces of our feelings that are part of this journey.

Color Your Feelings

If reading about the heartbreaking news of our damaged relationship with the natural world makes you are sad, scared, or angry, you're not alone. These are natural, healthy reactions to grief and loss, and it's healthy to express them.

For this exercise, you'll need five pages in your journal or five sheets of paper and some crayons, markers, colored pencils, or paint. You can also choose to cut pictures out of magazines and glue together a collage instead of drawing. Whatever materials you want to work with, make sure there are lots of choices of colors.

At the top of each page, write out these five partial sentences:

1. Some of the things I love most about nature are . . .
2. I feel the saddest when I hear about . . .
3. I sometimes get angry when I think about . . .

4. I get scared when I read that . . .

5. The thing I'm most excited about getting involved in helping is . . .

Complete the statements with pictures instead of words. You don't have to draw people or animals realistically if you don't want to: Sometimes just colors and shapes can express feelings. Are you attracted to bright colors like red and orange and bold jagged lines when you're mad? Do drops of darker colors like blue or grey match your feelings of sadness? You'll be expressing your own unique feelings and your own ways of communicating them, and however you choose to do that is the right way. Let yourself experiment with how to express yourself.

CLIMATE REFUGEES

Newtok village in Alaska has been home to the Yup'ik, the largest group of native Alaskans, for more than 2,000 years. The village is a beautiful mixture of modern and ancient ways. They still dry salmon and herring in wooden sheds like they've done for 1,000 years, but you'll also hear the roar of snowmobiles and ATV four-wheelers. But the melting Arctic ice has caused the seawater to creep up into this seaside village, and it's being submerged. The Yup'ik can no longer hold back against the rising water, and the town is now being forced to move away from the land where many generations of families were born and grew up. When people are uprooted and forced to abandon their homes and land due to climate change, they're called **climate refugees**.

A Pause for Empathy

Empathy is the ability to "put yourself in someone else's shoes" so that you can know how others might be feeling and understand their point of view. Practicing empathy helps you know how your actions affect others and what actions you may want to take to be a teammate or a friend. It helps you understand more about the people and the world around you, which is especially important as we join with all kinds of people to correct climate change.

Imagine what it would be like if you and your family and neighbors were forced to move away from a place you love and enjoy because it's threatened by water or fire. What would you be feeling? Can you relate to any of the types of grief you've read about in this chapter? Take a moment to write about it in your journal or on a sheet of paper.

The Yup'ik aren't the only community facing a radical change. Many of the most beautiful islands in the world are barely above sea level, which leaves them extremely vulnerable to the rising seas. On Tuvalu Island between Hawai'i and Australia, saltwater has saturated the land and made it difficult to grow traditional crops and find fresh drinking water. The half-million inhabitants of the Maldives, a string of islands off the coast of India and far out in the ocean, are also having to consider migration. Even a small rise in the sea level would engulf much of their living areas.

In 2010, Pakistan had severe flooding that affected 20 million people and drove millions from their homes. Almost a quarter of the food harvest for the year was washed away. While some people were able to return and rebuild, many people had to live in crowded camps without clean drinking water, which led to lots of disease and deaths.

You may have heard about Hurricane Katrina, which wiped out entire sections of New Orleans in 2005. More than 1,500 people died, and 15 years later there are still neighborhoods in the city that haven't been rebuilt. Most of New Orleans sits below sea level, so it will be at risk for even more of these kinds of problems, especially with the usual seasonal hurricanes becoming more intense and more frequent due to climate change. These are just a few of the examples of places where climate change is being felt right now.

Empathy in Action

If these kinds of disasters and recovery efforts were happening in your neighborhood, how would you want to help? Would you want to donate food or clothing, or take time to talk? Take five minutes to write or draw your answer in your journal or on a sheet of paper.

10,000 Joys and 10,000 Sorrows

You have been learning about many of the painful aspects of climate change, and in Chapter 5 you will also be reading about some exciting ways we are solving some of these problems and creating a healthier world together. There's a wise saying from long ago that's a good reminder for us today: "In every moment there are 10,000 joys and 10,000 sorrows." Our joys and sorrows aren't meant to be literally counted; the quote means that wherever we put our attention, our feelings follow. Since you've just been reading about some of the "10,000 sorrows" caused by climate change, the feelings that follow may be sorrow and grief. It's part of resilience to remember that there are also "10,000 joys" available in this moment as well.

A Pause for Gratitude

Look around you. Can you name ten things in your life right now that make you happy or that you appreciate? What's going well? Take a moment to write about it in your journal or on a piece of paper. It can be a helpful exercise to end each day thinking and writing about wonderful moments you've experienced. Maybe a friend shared a lunch snack, a teacher helped you understand something confusing, or it was fun to read a book with one of your parents. Notice and write about how you feel when you remember these kinds of happy moments.

It can be challenging to keep an accurate perspective, and sometimes our fears take hold. The world is still beautiful in so many places, and there's still time to change the path we've been taking. You'll be reading about turning points in history that demonstrate how we human beings are able to learn and change for the better.

You're also learning how to take care of yourself so that instead of being overwhelmed by big feelings, you can express them (go back and feel your deep connection to nature, or color your feelings whenever you need to), and you'll use your growing toolkit full of practices like the butterfly hug and balloon breathing to keep yourself calm and focused. You'll find new ways to feel supported by joining with others to become part of a meaningful movement toward an eco-wise way of life for all the beings on this planet as you envision creative and positive change.

In the next chapter, you'll learn more about the interconnection of all living things, and how this web of life holds an important key to positive change.

Levi Draheim

Levi was inspired to become a climate activist at the age of seven, when his home town in Florida was flooded by a major hurricane. He also had trouble breathing because of toxic algae blooms nearby, and he watched the local sea turtle nesting sites disappear.

When Levi was 11, he and 20 other kids sued the United States government for allowing the use of fossil fuels when it had knowledge of the damage they were causing. Their lawsuit argued that the government's actions violated the basic human rights in the Constitution (our right to pursue life, liberty, and happiness is damaged by human-caused pollution or climate change) and the public trust doctrine, which tells the government to protect our planet's natural resources like water and air. Though they didn't win the lawsuit, Levi doesn't plan to stop challenging bad policies any time soon. He continues to work closely with Our Children's Trust, a nonprofit law firm that supports young people in their legal efforts to demand a healthy and stable climate. He also works with the Hip Hop Caucus, a climate advocacy group that partners with leading artists to communicate important issues through music and dance.

Levi suggests that kids find a local environmental group to join, or form their own if their town doesn't have one. Levi says that he gets inspiration and energy from seeing all the good work and all the good people coming together to tackle climate change.

Can you imagine joining with other kids to challenge unhealthy policies and laws? How would you feel? What environmental youth groups meet where you live?

chapter 3:

EVERY THING IS CONNECTED

Every single thing in the world is connected by an invisible web, and touching one delicate thread sends ripples throughout the entire net. In this chapter you'll be learning about the three kinds of interconnected webs that we're all a part of, and how every part affects all the other parts. We'll take a deeper look at ecosystems, the web of living things; at everyday interconnections, like how river water ends up flowing through your kitchen faucet and returns again to the stream; and at teachings from Indigenous peoples who have understood our place in the web of life for thousands of years. When we realize that everything belongs in the web of life, including us, and that everything we do either helps or harms this web, we're naturally able to make more eco-wise choices.

About 60% of our bodies is made up of water, the very same water found in rivers, lakes, oceans, and rain. The sky enters our bodies through our breath in the form of oxygen and other gases, and some parts of our breath have at one time or another been part of other living things. Human beings all share 99.9% of the same DNA, the programming within cells that determines how every living thing will look and function, and we're also very closely related to many of our furry friends: Great apes share 98.8% of the same DNA with us, and even mice share almost 90%. Our bodies are made up of lots of the different things we can find on Earth, and they need over 60 elements—like iodine and iron that are found in rocks and soil—in order to be healthy. These elements usually become part of us through the food we eat. Is it surprising to you that the chemicals in rocks and soil are some of the same elements found in the human body? When we recognize these connections, it's easier to understand how our health and well-being are so closely tied to the health of our land, air, and water.

TWO CINQUAINS

A cinquain is a non-rhyming five-line poem that's arranged in a special way. Writing your observations in poetry is a fun way to help you develop a flexible mind for problem-solving and express your ideas, feelings, and solutions in new and creative ways. You'll be writing two poems. Give the first one the title "Eco-Anxiety," and write about the fears that come up for you about climate change. The second one you'll call "Web," and describe your personal experience of how all life is connected and how this awareness can help us work together to create a healthier world.

In your journal or on a sheet of paper, write your poems using the steps below. You can check out the examples below to get some ideas, too.

1. Title (use the ones given)

2. Two words that describe the title

3. Three interesting action words that fit the topic, ending in -ing

4. A four-word phrase the captures your feelings about the topic

5. One word, related to the title

Eco-Anxiety	Web
scared, questions	relationships, threads
trying, hoping, wondering	touching, connecting, holding
I hold my breath	bringing us all together
worried	whole

ECOSYSTEMS

Ecosystems are communities that consist of many different living things like plants, animals, and people all living in balance with each other and their environment—the air, water, soil, and temperature. All the parts of an ecosystem have learned how to rely on each other over time. Because the parts can't exist separately from each other, they're interdependent: They need each other to survive. And the greater the diversity in an ecosystem (the more different kinds of plants and animals and elements there are) the healthier the ecosystem. Just like everything else, we humans are part of the ecosystem, and we are dependent on thriving ecosystems for clean water to drink, places to grow nutritious food, and trees, rocks, and soil to build our homes and communities.

Biologists study water ecosystems like lakes, rivers, and oceans and land ecosystems like deserts, forests, and jungles. Even bacteria and other one-celled organisms organize themselves into mini ecosystems called microbiomes. The microbiome in your body includes bacteria and other organisms in places like your skin, teeth, and your gut, forming one community that works together to support your health. All the different ecosystems on our planet, from a microbiome to an ocean, are threads in the larger web of life on Earth, which is one big ecosystem made up of all the smaller ones. When it comes to the effects of climate change, if one ecosystem starts to falter, it can start a critical chain reaction that affects all the other ecosystems across the planet.

Let's look at the role of honeybees as an example of how ecosystems work, and we'll also learn about the effects that climate change is having on them. Bees have been around as far back as we know. Cave paintings in Spain show beekeeping dating back to 7,000 BCE.

Fossils of honeybees have been discovered that are 150 million years old!

If you bite into a juicy piece of watermelon this summer, you can thank the bees for it. Honeybees pollinate over one-third of our food, including almonds, apples, cherries, and broccoli. As bees fly from one flower to another, they distribute the grains of pollen that have stuck to their fuzzy bodies, and most plants need this new pollen to reproduce and create food. Bees also pollinate 90% of the wild plants that produce the seeds, nuts, and berries eaten by wild animals. But bees don't just help grow food: They are food. Several kinds of birds eat bees, including purple martins and the ruby-throated hummingbird, and so do insects like dragonflies and praying mantises.

Bees also help create wildlife **habitats**, because willows, poplars, and other trees can't grow without being pollinated by bees. Even in your own neighborhood there are hundreds of creatures, from birds and squirrels to thousands of tiny insects, that are helped by bees to eat and have a place to live in plants and trees. Without bees, our plates would be emptier and our gardens less beautiful, and animals that depend on these plants for survival would disappear.

In the late 20th century, biologists began noticing a drastic drop in the North American honeybee population, and in 2006 this trend was named "colony collapse disorder" (because honeybees live in groups called "colonies," and whole colonies were dying

at once). Between 750,000 and 1,000,000 colonies died in the United States over the winter of 2007–2008 alone, which was a loss of roughly 36% of all the bees in the country in just one season. Scientists have discovered five ways that climate change and pollution are causing major problems for our buzzing friends.

1. The honeybee habitat is shrinking because humans are using more and more of the planet to live on.

2. Bees are confused by the changes in seasons caused by climate change, and in some places

they're arriving too late for the short period of time when plants can be pollinated and reproduce.

3. Bee diseases increase in a warmer climate, and there's also an increase in mites and parasites that destroy hives.

4. Some common **pesticides** we use in farming are toxic to bees.

5. Bees don't always get the diverse diet they need to stay healthy, especially when farmers move hives in order to pollinate a single crop.

In 2019, the Environmental Protection Agency in the United States banned the use of 12 kinds of pesticides that kill bees, although the President later overturned the ban. (There is a lot of conflict between businesses wanting to make money and the kinds of laws that would support planetary health. That's why many of the kids you are reading about are taking legal action to enforce policies for an eco-wise society.) Luckily there's some good news about our tiny helpers, too. The bee population is on the rise again thanks to responsible farmers who are eliminating or reducing their pesticide use, and to more attention being paid to mite infestations. The European Union was successful in passing a total ban on the pesticides that harm bees in 2018. This is the kind of awareness, education, and action we can build on to help restore balance to our ecosystems.

It's easy to imagine how other winged, finned, and furry creatures are facing similar challenges as their habitats change because of climate change.

DOING THE DOGGIE SHAKE

Hearing about how climate change is harming bees can be upsetting and scary. But we can learn ways of coping from our animal and insect friends! Animals in the wild have often been observed releasing stress from a frightening experience by literally "shaking it off." After a big scare, animals shake for a brief period, followed by a deep, slow exhalation, and then they go about their day. Researchers believe that the shaking provides a healthy re-boot to their nervous system. As members of the animal kingdom, "shaking it off" is helpful to us, too!

Have you seen the way a wet dog dries itself off with a shimmy-shake that starts with its head and travels to its tail, with drops spraying everywhere in a flying halo of water? We're going to imitate this doggie action to "shake off" some of our own stress.

Stand up and give it a try. It's meant to feel a little silly, and you might even find yourself laughing:

1. Stand with your feet shoulder-distance apart. Begin gently shaking just your head from side to side and up and down, for about 10 seconds.

2. Now let your head rest, but keep the shaking going in your shoulders.

3. After about 10 seconds, let the shaking travel into your arms and hands, as if you were flicking water off your fingers.

4. Let the shaking move to your torso, moving your ribcage and hips as much as feels good.

5. Now let the shaking travel down each leg one at a time, 10 seconds for each, lifting your foot off the floor as if you're flicking water from the toes, then shaking the whole leg.

6. Repeat the doggie-shake six times head to toes, each time increasing the speed just a little until the last shaking moves through your body as one quick, shimmering flow.

7. Now pause and take a deep, slow breath in, and then exhale slowly and completely.

How do you feel?

The River in Your Kitchen Sink

We know that our drinking water comes from . . . somewhere. And when it goes down the drain, it goes . . . somewhere else. When you learn to connect the "somewheres," you'll find another interconnected system that we rely on.

There are two places our fresh water comes from: water on the Earth's surface in lakes, rivers, and streams, or groundwater that's usually found 100 to 500 feet below the surface in underground reservoirs called "aquifers." If you live on a farm or a rural area, you probably use underground water that's pumped up from a well on your property. If you live in a city or small town, you most likely get your water from the public supply company (which might draw water from either surface or underground water). After the water is analyzed and treated with chemicals for safety, it's pumped through a complex system of pipes and then pours through your faucet. But creating safe drinking water comes with challenges. Let's look at the example of what happened in Flint, Michigan.

In 2014, 100,000 people in Flint who used water from the city's utility company began getting bad-smelling, discolored water that caused itchy skin rashes and hair loss. At the same time, doctors discovered high levels of lead (a harmful type of metal) in many of the town's children's blood tests. Scientists discovered that chemical pollutants like lead were getting into the water from the city's old pipes. The

30,000 kids in Flint suffered the most, because lead can damage children's developing brains and nervous systems. Many children got sick. Some continue to struggle with a wide range of physical, mental, and emotional problems, and some have permanent brain damage.

While many people have heard about the Flint water crisis because it was in the news a lot, it's only one example of many areas that struggle to get clean water. Other pollutants in our public water come from oil pipelines, **fracking** (natural gas being forced to the surface from below ground using heavy machinery, high pressure, and chemicals), and pesticides that flow from farms into nearby streams and groundwater.

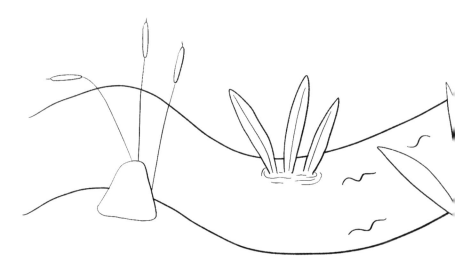

Once water leaves our homes from our laundry rooms, toilets, sinks, and showers, it goes back to the wastewater facilities to be treated and filtered again, and then it's usually returned to nearby rivers or oceans. But it's hard to get all the contamination out of the water. Imagine putting a single drop of red food-coloring into a glass of water. Now try to remove it. That's not so easy. Basically, the more pollutants get into our water systems, the harder it is to get them out and ensure safe drinking water.

One example is **microplastics**—tiny bits of plastic that are often too small to see. Every time we wash synthetic clothing, they shed microplastics: A fleece jacket alone sheds about 2,000 small pieces of plastic per washing. These tiny pieces of plastic get into

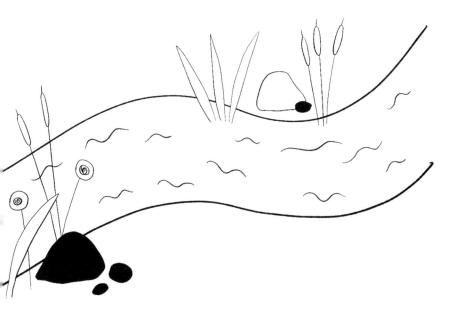

water sources like rivers, lakes, and oceans through the water cycles you've read about. Microplastics are found in the stomachs of creatures living in the deepest ocean trenches, in the rainfall atop the remote Pyrenees Mountains in southern France, and in Arctic snow and ice. There's virtually nowhere on Earth that's free of these particles because of how our ecosystems are interconnected.

Calming Down the "YIKES!"

Should you stop drinking the water that comes from your faucet? Probably not. Most of the country's drinking water is considered safe. Learning about what can happen to urban and rural water systems doesn't mean something's happening in your community right now, but it's important to learn about these problems so we can repair them and prevent future ones. It can be easy to believe the worst based on a little bit of information, and in this case sometimes our minds work against us instead of helping us.

When we hear scary news, it's natural to worry that we, and those we care about, might be in harm's way. Remember in the Introduction you learned that fear tries to protect us, but it's sometimes out of balance? As you read about four of the many ways our minds can trick us into believing something that isn't really true, notice if you sometimes have this kind of thinking. If so, be kind to yourself: It's natural for our thoughts to get out of balance with worry. The good news is that you can explore and adjust your thinking so that it is more accurate. You don't have to believe the thoughts that are untrue. Let's see how this applies to learning about climate change:

1. **Overgeneralization**: You come to a big conclusion based on a little bit of evidence. For example, someone who overgeneralizes might believe that they're a terrible student and should quit school because they did poorly on just one test. When it comes to pollutants, after reading about Flint they might assume that *all* water provided through public utility systems is unsafe to drink.

2. It's a **Catastrophe**: This is a mental habit of expecting that disaster is just around the corner; our mind always imagines the worst. The student with one poor grade might start worrying that they'll be expelled from school. In terms of climate change, you might spend a lot of time with "what if" scenarios: What if my house floods? What if I it gets too hot where I live? With this mental habit, it's your mind that's flooding, not your house.

3. It's All My Fault: This means you might take responsibility for the pain and happiness of everyone around you. In daily life, this person

may wonder, "Why are you unhappy? What did I do?" If they're focusing on climate change, rather than trying to learn ways to help, the person might begin to believe that it's up to them to solve *all* the world's challenges.

4. All or Nothing: Situations are viewed as extremes. People are either for us or against us. There's no room for the mixed feelings we explored in Chapter 1. In the example of climate change, you might bounce back and forth between thinking that we live in an ideal world or that we're all doomed. It's impossible to find a middle ground that sees climate problems realistically and understands that we can strive to make improvements that will take time to have an impact.

Our thoughts and feelings are closely connected, and when our thinking becomes exaggerated by fear, it keeps us feeling bad by increasing our stress and depression.

GETTING TO KNOW YOUR MENTAL HABITS

In your journal or on a piece of paper, write down the name of the four thought habits described above. Under each one, write another example of a climate change-related thought that would fit the description of that habit, and a feeling that would go along with that thought. Then write down a "More True" statement that's more accurate, along with a different feeling. Here's an example:

1. Overgeneralization: My best friend doesn't recycle. That means people don't really care about climate change.

2. Feeling: This makes me sad and angry.

3. More True: I know a lot of other people who recycle. Maybe my friend doesn't know about the benefits of recycling. I'm going to talk to her about it and see what happens.

4. Feeling: More hopeful.

Which of these kinds of thinking seem familiar to you? Like the way we identified feelings of sadness and grief so that you could work with those feelings, it's also very helpful to increase your awareness of the ways your mind can trick you so you can correct them and find a more accurate perspective.

Indigenous Earth-Wise Traditions

"Indigenous people" refers to many different groups and First Peoples around the world who lived in their particular geographical area for thousands of years before other cultures moved in and established a different—and usually dominant—society. The colonizers often used brutal violence to force Indigenous people to follow different laws and practices, often through forced migration, slavery, and violence. Today there are more than 370,000,000 Indigenous people with a vast range of unique traditions, languages, and practices spread across 70 countries. Just a few examples include the Native American Hopi and Sioux in North America, the Maya in Mexico and parts of South America, the Inuit in Arctic regions, the Sami in Northern Europe, and the Maori in New Zealand. Each of these communities has their own special characteristics, cultures, and beliefs, but many Indigenous teachings have similar views about the interconnected nature of life. We can learn from these teachings to understand the web of life and reduce the damage we're doing to the Earth.

The Earth is seen as a living, active being in many Indigenous communities. If we live with this awareness, it naturally guides our choices in a different way. The flow of life through the web is also called the Great Circle or the Hoop of Life by some Indigenous people. Chief Si'ahl, or Chief Seattle, a Suquamish and Duwamish chief (1786–1866) is often credited with this essential perspective: "Humanity has not woven the web of life. We are but one thread within it. Whatever we do to the web, we do to ourselves. All things are bound together. All things connect."

We can learn from such eco-wise traditions to take greater care even with simple everyday items in order to reduce waste and conserve natural resources. For example, rather than seeing a wooden chair as just another object, we can recognize that the wood came from a living tree that was nourished by the rain, sun, and air, all the essential elements in the Earth's ecosystem. From an Indigenous perspective, each of these natural elements are often considered sacred. There is an attitude of appreciation for all that went into the creation of that wooden chair: It's made of the Earth itself, but it's also been touched by many beings before it came into your home. Imagine the chair's journey. Where did the tree originally grow, and what kind of tree was it? What creatures made their home in it and took shelter under its branches? How many people's lives contributed to creating your chair? Once the chair grows rickety from use, imagine it returning to the forest where it came from, the wood naturally decomposing into soil and supporting the lives of the surrounding trees. Then, the circle of life is complete.

The Life Cycle of a Chair

Choose a chair you often use in your home and explore what you can learn about its life cycle. If you're not sure, ask a family member where it came from. Are there any tags that might offer information about where it was made? If the chair you have came from Turkey or Vietnam, did you know that it might have been built by children your age or even younger? What materials are in your chair: fabric, wood, plastic, metal? Once the chair is broken, or no longer needed or wanted, where will it go? How likely is it that it would eventually end up in a dump?

Even if you can't find out all the answers about the life cycle of your chair, imagine the likely steps of the production and transportation systems used in getting this chair to you, and where it may be in the future.

How does the story of your chair compare to the life cycle of the wooden chair you read about? What feelings come up when you consider the differences? Take time to write about your feelings in your journal or on a piece of paper.

When we learn to understand the natural resources people are using, we'll more naturally feel gratitude and consider how we can be part of restoring a sustainable world. One of the big contributors to climate change is a lack of balance: We've over-used our planet's natural resources at a rate faster than their ability to be replenished, putting increasing pressure on biodiversity and the health of ecosystems. As Chief Jacqueline Thomas of the Saik'uz First Nation reminds us, "The land takes care of us when we take care of the land."

One of the ways we can actively remember the Circle of Life and live in greater harmony with the environment is through our language. Other people, animals, plants, and natural elements are referred to in many Indigenous traditions as family: "All my relations," "Our four-legged brothers and sisters," "Plant beings," or "Finned and flying beings." We naturally want to care for and protect our family, and if we expand our definition of family to include all of nature, we'll become more caring toward our environment. Changing the quality of our relationship to the environment, to others, and to ourselves is at the heart of the solution to our climate problems.

Scientific and Indigenous worldviews offer us different ways of exploring eco-wise living. While we can't know in advance how our societies will evolve and change as we begin to apply scientific, cultural, and everyday solutions to climate change, we can use them all as guiding principles for the eco-wise choices we'll be making.

Grounding

You've learned that you're literally made of all the elements of life, and research is showing that the more time you spend in nature—in direct contact with fresh air, sunlight, and the ground under your feet—the healthier you'll be. Give it a try.

The basic exercise is simple: Go outside, take off your shoes, and stand barefoot on the ground. There are lots of easy variations: Sit on the ground outdoors in a park or natural place and eat lunch, read a book, or hang out with friends. Lie on your back and watch the clouds. Your direct contact with the Earth will do all the work.

In some neighborhoods it's more challenging to find comfortable outdoor areas, so if that's true for you, start with the natural elements that are easily available. Go to a window where you can see the sky. Notice the colors. Can you see clouds or sunlight, or hear birds, wind, or insects? On a rainy day, notice how the smell of the air changes. Imagine the earth that is under the floor and building. On a computer, look at videos of forests, jungles, deserts, beaches— whatever you are curious about. Imagine what it might feel like to be there with all the colors, textures, scents, sounds, and feel of the air, and the Earth under your feet.

Some studies are saying that being outdoors for 20 minutes a day twice a day gives us a wide range of health benefits: improved circulation, getting sick less often, and a better mood. Pick a clean, clear spot where it's safe to relax . . . and go relax in person or your imagination!

MINDFUL GROUNDING

You can reap the benefits of being outdoors even more if you add a mindfulness practice. Mindfulness is really paying attention to and appreciating the moment you're in. Outdoors, this can mean intentionally focusing on your environment in a way that quiets your mind and helps you connect more deeply with nature. You can do this with your eyes closed or partly open. It goes like this:

Spend about one minute with each of these four steps. If you notice your thoughts start wandering and getting distracted, just recognize that it's happening and let them go, then return to the exercise:

1. Notice the sounds in your environment. Just listen: Maybe you'll hear a breeze in the leaves, the hum of an insect, or a car passing by. Listen to sounds as close to you as your own breath, to the sounds around you, and to sounds that are far away.

2. Now focus on all the places where your body feels the contact with the Earth. If you're sitting up, it might

be parts of your hips, legs, and feet. If you're lying down, it could be all along your back, head, arms, and legs. Focus on feeling the light pressure of your body's contact with the ground, on feeling the warmth or coolness, or the subtle sensations like tingling or numbness. . . . There aren't any specific sensations you should be having; this exercise is just about noticing the sensations you're actually having as you're having them. Whatever you feel is okay.

3. Notice any scents in the air: pleasant, not-so-nice, or neutral. Now become aware of any tastes in your mouth.

4. In the last step, place your attention on how you feel emotionally. Again, this is an awareness exercise, and there's no need to change anything. Just be present with yourself and what you're noticing.

Poetic Grounding

For one more variation, read these song lyrics like a poem and let yourself go on a journey of imagination for a few minutes. If possible, try this outdoors while standing barefoot on the ground:

"Put your roots down, put your feet on the ground, can you hear what She says if you listen? The sound of the river as it moves across the stones is the same sound as it moves in your body as it moves across your bones. Are you listening? Are you listening?"

If the Earth had a voice, what might she be expressing to you right now? Write or draw in your journal or a piece of paper any image, thought, feeling, or inspiration that comes to you as you listen.

While climate change is touching the entire planet because our ecosystems are so interconnected, it's not affecting every place equally right now. You'll read next about climate justice, and how it's often the people who are least responsible for emitting CO_2 into the atmosphere who are the first to feel the effects of the climate crisis.

Autumn Peltier

Autumn was eight years old and attending a water ceremony a few miles from her home when she saw signs posted everywhere that said, "Don't drink or touch the water." Her mother explained that on 56 of the First Nation reservations in Canada, the water was so contaminated that it was unsafe, mostly due to leaking oil pipelines. Autumn has been a fierce "water protector" ever since, advocating for the universal right to clean drinking water.

Autumn is Anishinaabe-kwe and a member of the Indigenous Wiikwemkoong First Nation, and she lives in Unceded Anishinaabe Territory on Manitoulin Island in northern Ontario, Canada. When she was 12, she presented Canadian Prime Minister Justin Trudeau with the traditional gift of a copper water pot as a symbol of her community's need for drinkable water. That got the world's attention, and it prompted the Assembly of First Nations to create a scholarship fund that would allow Autumn to attend international gatherings like the Children's Climate Conference in Sweden.

While she's very committed to continuing her work as a water warrior, Autumn admits that she's struggled. She's cried about the First Nation communities that can't drink their own water, one of the most sacred elements in their culture. She also suffered a lot of bullying because of her activism. But as we've seen with so many youth leaders, one sincere action often leads to another larger one. Autumn has now spoken to the United Nations Assembly multiple times, she's been nominated for the 2019 International Children's Peace Prize, and she was named one of the most inspiring and influential women by the British Broadcasting Corporation.

Have you ever had an important moment that awakened your environmental passion?

chapter 4:

PRACTICING

ECO-JUSTICE

Environmental justice, climate justice, or simply eco-justice: These terms describe how our environmental problems are connected to many social issues, including racial discrimination, human rights abuses, poverty, and the unfair distribution of necessary resources. People who are concerned with eco-justice also understand how those who are least responsible for global warming often suffer the worst consequences of environmental pollution and climate change. Some people even can't get the most basic resources. While all areas on the planet will be affected by the climate crisis, the world's poorest people will bear the heaviest burden, from rising seas and intense droughts to shortages of water and food.

Eco-justice addresses "environmental racism," which explains how companies often build toxic waste facilities or polluting factories in areas where people of color live. Those residents aren't included in decisions about their neighborhood or in city leadership positions. This is part of **systemic racism** or "institutional racism," which means that there are many government policies, ideas, and actions that provide an unjust amount of resources to white people while denying them to people of color.

You read about the water crisis in Flint, Michigan. Many people believe that the government's slow response to fix the problem was because the community is made up of 63% people of color, mostly Black Americans. In addition, about 40% of the community lives below the poverty line. Dan Kildee, a government representative in Flint, is one of many who believe that race is the single biggest cause of what happened there. But these kinds of problems aren't limited to Flint: for example, research shows that in the United States as a whole, lead poisoning is five times more common among Black children than White children, mostly because of old pipes in less expensive housing.

Racial discrimination means being unfairly burdened by a lack of safe and healthy environmental choices, and it creates painful experiences that increase eco-anxiety, anger, frustration, and sadness. Because of the ways that racism is built into our society, there's often unequal treatment and a lack of dignity and respect in daily life, and that creates many stressful experiences. We'll be taking a deeper look at environmental racism and the feelings that it triggers, and we'll practice some ways to work through those feelings and clarify your own values so you can be part of a just solution.

Social Systems and Eco-Justice

Just like everything in our planet's ecosystems is connected, each part of our social system is also connected by threads in an invisible web: Every part affects every other part and that affects the whole. Most institutions, including the law, schooling, the economy, healthcare, the business world, and the government are still blemished by our shameful past with its immoral treatment of Black Americans, Indigenous Americans, and other people of color. For example, people of color have historically had a harder time getting a high-quality education. That's because schools in the communities where they live unfairly receive less money from the government, so the schools don't have as many resources and opportunities. Having poor educational choices can narrow a person's job options, which often leads to earning a lower income. With less money, people have fewer housing and food choices. Nobody wants to live in an area that contains a toxic dump or that's more likely to flood—but not everyone has the money to easily move to a safer area. In these communities, making eco-wise choices is more difficult or even impossible. For example, buying and eating organic food helps the environment and our own health by reducing pollution from pesticides and the amount of toxins we eat—and it's also more expensive. In stores in lower-income communities, organic foods might not only be more expensive, they might not even be for sale.

A Pause for Feelings— Eco-Justice

You're learning that feelings tell you something— right now it may be that people or places need to be protected or restored. Our feelings go hand-in-hand with our climate justice actions. Have you experienced discrimination or other kinds of injustice? What other situations of injustice have you seen or heard about? In your journal or on a piece of paper, write about your experiences and the feelings that go with them. You might be tempted to write about possible solutions, but take time with your feelings first.

Global Climate Injustice

These kinds of inequalities don't just stay within the borders of the United States; there is injustice on a global scale when it comes to climate change. For example, the atmosphere that surrounds our planet belongs to everyone. "Atmospheric Colonization" describes a situation where central systems of power unfairly dominate the resources by excessive carbon emissions. That is exactly what has happened. Higher-income places in the Northern hemisphere, including the United States, Europe, Canada, Japan, and Australia, are responsible for 92% of global emissions. The United States alone is responsible for 40%! This means that the global South, including Latin America, Africa, and the Middle East, are only responsible for 8%. And yet the global South has far fewer resources to recover from the losses due to droughts, floods, storms, and wildfires caused by climate change. Many who study these impacts believe that higher income countries owe a climate debt to the rest of the world.

The large-scale damage and destruction of nature that is taking place globally is legally permitted in many parts of the world. This legal damage to the planet is called "ecocide." This includes things like the bee-killing pesticides that you've read about, but also the dumping of cancer-causing pollution into rivers, air and ocean contamination from nuclear testing, cutting down Amazon jungles to raise cattle, mountaintop removal to mine coal, and many more. These practices create injustices for communities that live near highly-impacted areas, and are aggressive assaults from corporate and political policies and laws that harm our entire interconnected living system.

THAT'S NOT FAIR!

When you realize that things in life can be given or taken away based only on factors like where a person was born, the color of their skin, their gender, or their physical appearance, you might think, "That's not fair!" And you'd be right. Eco-justice tells us that if we're going to work together to create a healthier world, we also need to work to heal our unjust society at the same time. When we realize that our social systems and institutions are unfair, it often brings up uncomfortable feelings. You might feel angry, sad, confused, scared, guilty, frustrated, or more. This next exercise will help you to feel how difficult it can be to live a life that's limited in opportunities to thrive. You could already have upsetting feelings around social injustice, or it might be surprising to you to learn that you have a more privileged life. As hard as it might be to understand, we don't all start out with the same opportunities and resources.

OPPORTUNITIES EXPERIMENT

1. Write your full name on a page in your journal or on a sheet of paper.

2. Now write it again, but this time use your non-dominant hand: If you're left-handed, use your right hand, and if you're right-handed, use your left.

3. Write your full name a third time using your non-dominant hand with your eyes closed.

4. Compare the names. When you first wrote your name, you had all your strengths and resources available to guarantee the best possible result. The second time might have been more challenging, because you were trying to do something that you're not experienced or comfortable with. The third time removed another key element of success. How did these differences affect what you were trying to create?

5. How you would feel if you injured your dominant hand and had go through your day using your non-dominant hand, or performing certain activities blindfolded? Take a moment to imagine a few examples, and then write about your feelings.

6. Now apply this exercise to your daily life. Are there unfair situations where your opportunities are blocked or are less available to you than other

people? Notice what feelings come
up when you think about your life
experiences. Write about your feelings
in your journal or on a piece of paper.
Make room for all the feelings, big
and small.

If this exercise describes situations you don't relate
to or haven't thought much about, take time now
to imagine how challenging it would be if your most
important decisions or life experiences were limited:
for example, if you didn't have an easy way to get
clean drinking water or nutritious food. Write about
your feelings.

Anger and Sadness Are Close Cousins

You might have noticed that the Opportunities Experiment triggered feelings that included anger, sadness, or both. These feelings are natural reactions to an experience where you, someone you care about, or something you believe in has been hurt or wronged. It's common for us to move back and forth between the two feelings.

Sometimes it's easier to be angry, especially if you've been told the inaccurate message that "sadness is weakness" or "boys don't cry," or if you're so sensitive that feeling sadness is hard to bear and you feel extremely vulnerable. Or maybe it's difficult to be angry because you're growing up in a household with an angry parent, and that emotion feels dangerous. Or it could be just the opposite: a household where anger, even when it's justified, isn't allowed.

It can take time to sort out our feelings, but it's worth it. Feelings are a gift; they're natural for everyone to have and they give us different ways to understand a difficult or unjust situation. A good way to start is when you're feeling angry, to pause and ask yourself if you're feeling any sadness, too. And when you're sad, take a deeper look to sense whether anger is part of your full reaction. Anger is especially helpful in eco-justice, because it can fuel your decision to speak up and stand up for equality. But it takes some emotional skills to make that work. If an angry impulse causes you to aggressively attack, it could end up harming you or others and have the opposite result: your desire for justice might be seen by others as violent or just rude.

Think of an unjust situation right now that gets you really angry. Following the steps below, imagine how it would be to try out the "STOP skill" the next time you face that challenge.

The STOP Skill

S Stop: Simply pause what you're doing. You might feel like lashing out or running away, but practice building the muscle of "pausing before you act."

T Take a step back: take three deep breaths, and while you're doing it, put your attention on the feeling of the air entering your nose and expanding your lungs, and then feel it leaving your body as you exhale.

O Observe yourself: Notice the thoughts in your mind, notice your feelings, and feel the sensations in your body.

P Proceed thoughtfully: What's the best thing to say or do right now? Would that be likely to lead to the outcome you want to create? What would be most successful and appropriate?

OUR INTERNAL ECOSYSTEM AND ECO-JUSTICE

Our personal values, thoughts, actions, health, and feelings create our very own ecosystem. Our values and beliefs guide our actions and our behavior, and that affects how we feel. For example, if you believe that everyone deserves respect, and you see a kid at school being teased for the way they look, you might decide to act on your values by speaking out and saying, "Stop it, not cool." Or you could change the situation by saying, "We've got to get to class, come on," and walking away with the person. If your actions match your values, you'll feel good about yourself and the situation. Imagine how you might feel if you stood by or turned away.

When your actions are consistent with your values and your feelings, it's called **integrity**: Your personal ecosystem is in harmony, and nothing inside feels out of balance. It's not always easy and not always possible in every situation, but every healthy action makes a difference. Do you spend time thinking about how your personal choices influence the larger world? Social rights activist Desmond Tutu reminds us that, "If you are neutral in situations of injustice, you have chosen the side of the oppressor." Let's take a closer look at how your personal values can contribute to making our world healthier and more just for everyone.

Getting Clear on Your Values

Are you living in a way that matches what you think is important for creating a healthier planet and society? If you make your choices in harmony with your values, you become your best self, and then you have the potential to help the world be better than it is. You can't be perfect, and you can't solve it all by yourself, but you can explore how to contribute your gifts and talents to the different eco-wise movements that are important to you.

Being successful with our eco-wise goals starts with getting to know yourself by identifying your most deeply-felt values. The next step is patience and practice. It's like playing the piano, hitting a softball, or learning to cook. You get better over time and with experience. Follow the steps in the next exercise to identify your values and create eco-wise action steps toward your goals.

Being Your Best Eco-Wise Self

1. Read through the list of values and pick out the top five that are the most important to you. You can also add different values if you don't see

yours on the list. Using five sheets of paper or pages in your journal, write one of the qualities you picked at the top of each page, with number 1 as the most important value and 5 the least important (but being in the top 5 is still pretty darn important!). Value examples could be: Adventurous, Appreciative of Beauty, Authentic, Brave, Caring, Collaborative, Community-Oriented, Cooperative, Creative, Fair, Family-Centered, Freedom-Loving, Friendly, Healthy, Helpful, Honest, Humorous, Kind, Leading Others, Learning New Things, Living with Integrity, Loving, Open-Minded, Patient, Peaceful, Reasonable, Respectful, Responsible, Safe, Successful, Supportive, Trustworthy.

2. Under each of your five qualities, write a short definition of what the value means to you and how you can use it in eco-wise living.

3. Then add a "Step 1" that you can take this week to use that value in your eco-wise actions or behavior.

4. Describe how your life might look in one year if you continue with similar actions.

5. Do you need any support to get started? If so, how can you get that support?

6. Who will benefit from your environmental decisions and actions? Is there anything you want to change about your plan that could encourage others to be involved? How do you feel after writing out your values and your plans?

Here's an example:

◐ Creative: I value creativity and I love to draw. I want to use my art to help people learn more about keeping our oceans clean.

◐ For a first step, this week I'm going to create a poster about clean ocean actions. I'll talk to my science teacher to see if my poster can be put in the classroom or the hall.

◐ Over the next year, I'll see if there are any youth climate-action groups in the community that need help with posters for marches or educational programs where I could help.

◐ I'm a little shy and it would be easier if my friend joins me when I talk to my science teacher. I'll ask if he'll come with me.

- I wonder if there are other kids at my school who want to do something like this. I can ask and see about starting an after-school club where we could do activities like this together. Maybe we would come up with more ideas.
- I feel surprised that I'm excited about this! I'm a little nervous too, but I want to give it a try.

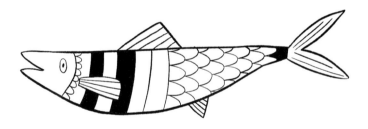

Diversity

The more diversity there is in an ecosystem, the more resilient it is. The system has a greater ability to bounce back from stress like pollution and adapt to change with a greater number and variety of species. This is also true when people come together to create thriving eco-wise communities. Societies are strongest and most resilient when there are a wide range of diverse gifts and talents that weave together in new and creative ways. For example, if your after-school eco-club has a lot of different kinds of cultures and personalities in the group, they'll come up with more interesting and varied ideas.

If you read a few other kids' "Being Your Eco-Wise Self" plans, you'd discover all kinds of smart ideas. Besides the example of art, some kids might start a school garden, explore how to reduce waste and increase recycling at their school, look for a mentor so they can learn more about a science career in environmental studies, or find out about local clean-energy policies. If you're not sure what you'd like to do, you might talk with an adult or search the internet for more ideas of things kids are doing for the environment. Because we live in an ecosystem, we need each other. Right now, we need to use every possible talent and activity to heal our planet from pollution, waste, and rising temperatures and help everyone learn how to live from an eco-wise perspective.

Our world is diverse: There are many seasons, careers, colors, textures, scents, ideas, cultures, skills, foods, beliefs, feelings, and more. The next exercise gives you a chance to reflect on a few of the important ideas you've been learning about and then engage in some creative expression—while also having fun with diverse objects, colors, and textures.

CREATIVE REFLECTION CIRCLE

1. Find a basket or bag or a muffin tin, which could be helpful for separating small items. Walk around your home or outdoors and collect things that in some way relate to the following four themes of your Circle. Here are a few examples of the kinds of things you might choose:

   ◐ Diversity: Collecting green, yellow, red, and brown leaves could be a reminder that life expresses itself beautifully in many different ways.

   ◐ Climate Change Feelings: A rock or piece of plastic could mean that "sometimes feelings are hard."

   ◐ Everything Is Connected: Pieces of string or twigs that connect the objects in your circle can remind you how all parts of nature need to work together to thrive.

   ◐ Our Amazing World: Perhaps a seed or pinecone represents how awesome it is that something as small as a seed grows to become a huge tree. A food item from your cupboard may include ingredients that grew in an open field, like wheat or corn, and remind you of the incredible journey it took to end up on your plate.

2. You might choose twigs, pebbles, seeds,
   a piece of foil, a button: anything goes.
   As long as the objects make sense to you,
   that's all that matters.

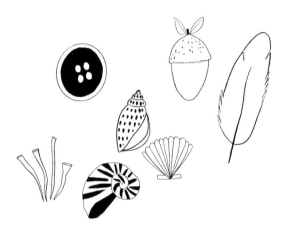

3. Find a smooth, flat surface outdoors
   on the ground or inside on the floor to
   create your Reflection Circle. Make
   sure that the area will be protected
   from things like wind and scampering
   dogs. Take your time, allowing at least
   20 minutes. The circle can be as large
   as you want.

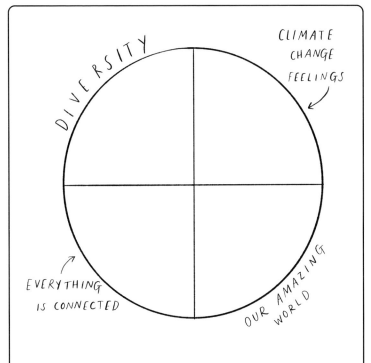

4. Create the circle using string or twigs or by placing the objects that you collected in a circle.

5. Divide the circle into four even sections, also using string, twigs, or objects. You can write the name of each theme on paper above each section or use the theme's initials.

6. Trust the creative process and have fun! There's no "right way" to do it. Think for a moment about how the object relates to the theme, and then place it in the section that matches best.

7. When you're done, step back and look at your Reflection Circle. What do you notice? What feelings come up? Take a few minutes and write about your experience in your journal or on a sheet of paper.

8. You can take a photo of your Circle to keep in your journal or notes. In the final step, return the objects you chose to their original places (unless they were litter!).

There are many variations of this exercise: You can draw the Reflection Circle on a piece of paper and glue objects to it, or use markers to draw things in each section, or you can paste pictures from magazines into your Circle to create a collage.

In the next chapter, you'll learn about people from around the world who are putting their values into action. They're making improvements to big systems that help build up healthier farming practices, innovative city designs, greener transportation options, wetland and park restoration, and so much more. The more we create change *together*, the more successfully we can turn climate change around.

Jaden Anthony, aka "Kid Brooklyn"

Comics can do a world of good! Ten-year-old Jaden from Brooklyn turned what he loved doing—drawing comics—into an educational and fundraising program focused on climate change and social justice. This was his way of acting on his desire to make the world a better place for everyone.

With the help of his Dad, Jaden started a crowdfunding page through Kickstarter, and he raised enough money to publish his first comic book series, Kid Brooklyn. It tells the stories of a young boy and his band of friends who use their superpowers to change the world. Each story describes a different environmental or social issue and gives tips on how to be part of the solution.

Jaden was first inspired to do something about the toxic water in Flint, Michigan, and he joined with the efforts of Greenforall.org. A portion of every comic he sells helps replace Flint's aging pipes and bring safe water to the families there.

It's important to Jaden for his characters to reflect the gender and ethnic diversity that's the reality in our country and throughout the world. He also brings science, technology, engineering, and math into his action-packed tales. Jaden knows that every kid can make a difference, and he wants you to know that too.

What's your superpower? How do you feel when you use your superpower to help make the world healthier and more just?

chapter 5

MAKING A HEALTHIER WORLD TOGETHER

Have you ever had one of those weeks that's full of fun—until you have an argument with a friend, and suddenly that's the only thing you can think about? The conflict might leave you feeling sad, worried, or mad, and those upsetting feelings seem like they've erased the all the happiness you just experienced. That's because our brains are wired with a **negativity bias**, which means that we're more sensitive to unpleasant news and events; we react more strongly to them, and we remember them longer than pleasant events. This can actually be helpful, because it gives us a chance to reflect on what went wrong and how we can do things differently next time. But it can also work against us unless we learn to balance it out by deliberately focusing on things that are going well in our personal lives and the world around us.

Negativity bias is usually active when you're learning about climate change, too. It can make you feel more overwhelmed when you hear the news about melting glaciers, the way animals in the wild are struggling, and how families are losing their homes to fire or floods. While there *are* many distressing things happening, it's not the whole picture. A healthy approach to studying climate change includes intentionally learning about the great advances being made. More than ever before, people are waking up to the importance of reversing climate change by doing things differently. There are many creative and exciting innovations happening right now that will lead to a safer and healthier world, and you can be part of that. This chapter highlights just a few of the many changes happening around the world.

DRAWDOWN

You've already learned that greenhouse gases in the atmosphere are the primary cause of the climate crisis. **Drawdown** is a term used to describe the goal of reaching a point in the near future where the level of greenhouse gases stops climbing and steadily declines as safely, quickly, and justly as possible. This would gradually reduce the global average temperature and stop the destructive effects of climate change. But before we read about the drawdown efforts others are making, let's start by envisioning your own creative ideas.

DREAM BOARD

A Dream Board is a creative way to organize your goals and intentions for the future using magazine pictures and quotes. Your Dream Board will reflect your personal eco-wise choices as you move forward in your life. It doesn't have to contain practical steps: Let yourself dream and imagine the safer and healthier world you want to see. For example, you might show bikes on the streets instead of cars, all kinds of people working together to grow a community garden full of vegetables, a forest filled with wildlife in a thriving ecosystem, or a futuristic city that runs completely on sustainable energy. This is a fun project to do with friends or your eco-club, with each person creating their own board, or you can do it on your own. Allow about 30 minutes for this exercise.

1. Assemble the materials. For the board, you can use a big piece of cardboard cut from a box, colorful construction paper, poster board—whatever's handy. Find some magazines that you can cut or tear pictures and quotes from. You can also use stickers and lightweight objects like leaves that will be easy to glue or tape down. Get glue, tape, marking pens, scissors, and any other materials you want to use. Or you can draw pictures of your own directly onto your board.

2. Browse through the magazines and start cutting or tearing out any pictures, words, and phrases that

appeal to you. You can decide later about which ones you'll actually use.

3. Begin to lay the pictures and words you like most on the board, without gluing or taping them down yet. They can be overlapping or intentionally messy, or you can arrange them in a more organized way. Move them around until you land on the arrangement that seems just right to you.

4. If there are any inspirational quotes or words you love that you didn't find in the magazines, write them directly on the board or on pieces of paper that you can then glue or tape to the board.

5. Complete your Dream Board by attaching all your pictures, quotes, and objects with glue or tape.

6. When it's complete, take a few minutes to really look at what you've made. How does it feel to imagine this better future you can help create?

7. Find a place to put the board in your room where it's one of the first and last things you see every day. You can always put a photo of it in your

journal if you want, or keep one on your phone. Over time, you can add more pictures and quotes so that your board grows right along with your new discoveries.

CIVIC ENGAGEMENT

So many positive changes have occurred through **civic engagement**, which are efforts that make positive contributions to the community. You've been learning how many of the things that cause climate change are woven into our society, from the ways we produce food, to transportation, to the legal guidelines for pollution. While it's important to explore how each one of us can do our part individually, civic engagement is important because we can accomplish even more as a group. For example, if a family installs solar panels on the roof of their home for sustainable energy, that's great. But if a whole city designates funds to build a solar farm to provide clean energy to all the households and businesses, the benefits really multiply.

John Lewis is a great example of a civic leader and climate justice advocate. He devoted more than 50 years working for the common good. He marched on the streets at the height of the civil rights movement and worked to pass more equitable laws as a congressman. In 1992, he introduced the first piece of legislation focused on the unfair impacts of pollution on communities of color: The Environmental Justice Act. The United States Environmental Protection Agency (EPA) later honored him with the "Environmental Justice Champion" award.

He knew his work continued the efforts from those who came before him, and he encouraged current generations to become agents of change. He offers us a few tips from his experience:

> It is my belief that our country needs better environmental protections and that real protections do not have to come at the expense of jobs or our economy. . . . I want to see young people in America feel the spirit of the 1960s and find a way to get in the way. To find a way to get into trouble. Good trouble, necessary trouble. . . . When you see something that is not right, not fair, not just, you have to speak up; you have to do something . . . if they don't give you a seat at the table, bring a folding chair.

Civic engagement is for all ages. At the height of the Civil Rights Movement, children and teenagers took part in the Children's March in 1963, walking downtown to talk to the mayor about segregation. This was an inspiration for the Children's March that took place in Seattle, Washington, in 2020, where nearly 3,000 turned out for a peaceful protest continuing the civil rights efforts of the Black Lives Matter movement.

Getting involved can take many forms: volunteering for an event that matters to you, writing letters to those in leadership positions, raising awareness through art or social media. There are many organizations you could join to learn more, and add your voice to the effort, such as signing up to be an Earth Protector (stopecocide.earth). As you continue exploring your feelings and talents, you will find the ways of participating that are a good match for you.

Clean Energy and Carbon Capture

According to researchers at Stanford University in California, we truly can change our climate situation. Engineers reviewed 47 scientific research studies by 91 authors, and all of them agreed that the technology already exists to achieve 100% renewable energy for all the world's energy needs using wind, solar, and water power. The only thing standing in the way of making this change right now is the lack of sweeping government policies that would support the transition from fossil fuel-based energy to renewable energy. But many places are still forging ahead and making progress. New Zealand passed a historic bill that plans to get the entire country down to zero carbon emissions by 2050. In the United States, Texas is taking the lead in wind power, now supplying the state with more

power from wind than coal. Wind power offers tremendous potential: Studies found that if wind farms were created in the North Atlantic Ocean, they would produce enough energy to supply all of humanity's electricity needs.

The benefits of electricity as a cleaner alternative to natural gas are catching on fast! Berkeley, California, became the first city to ban natural gas hookups in new construction, and soon Brookline Massachusetts, Los Angeles, San Francisco, and Seattle joined the "electrify everything" movement with various stages of pro-electric laws and policies underway. This is a global movement, with the United Kingdom also passing a new law that bans any new gas hookups for new homes starting in 2025.

We're not just looking at ways to reduce or eliminate pumping carbon into the atmosphere; some engineers are also studying ways to *remove* carbon dioxide from the air. One promising idea is planting vast underwater meadows of seagrass. Seagrass is able to absorb and store carbon, which then remains buried for hundreds of years. It's free, it's natural, it's exciting: Seagrass can store up to 100 times more than land-based ecosystems such as rainforests!

New Farming Practices

What if you could play Frisbee all day at the beach and then head home with bags of fresh groceries? That might be possible someday with the solar-powered floating farms now being designed by Forward Thinking Architecture. The farms float on lakes and oceans and use sunlight and rainwater in an aquaculture system that raises fish and grows plants together in water, rather than soil. They can grow up to 20 tons of vegetables per day! This is great news, especially for areas that don't have good soil or enough water for traditional farming. If this kind of farming can take off around the world, it would also reduce our need to import food, which would reduce carbon emissions even more by cutting down on shipping and trucking. The company designing these farms is getting ready to build the first trial farm in Singapore.

Not all innovations are new ideas! These floating farms use remarkably similar agricultural systems to the Aztec farming practice from the 1500s called *chinampas*. These "floating gardens" in Mexico were successfully created in lakes where the land was not suitable for growing crops.

Fresh Drinking Water

People have been trying to figure out how to take the salt out of ocean water to make it drinkable—a process called **desalination**—for a very long time, but it's always been too expensive or difficult . . . until now! A non-profit organization called Give Power built the world's first solar-powered desalination plant in Kenya. Using very efficient solar panels and batteries from Tesla, the sun is producing 20,000 gallons of clean drinking water there every day, enough for 35,000 people, at only a penny a gallon. Give Power is installing a second plant in a different Kenyan village, one in Haiti, and one in Columbia. The goal is to provide drinking water from the sea to even larger numbers of people, and this is a very exciting start.

Ocean Cleanup

About halfway between Hawai'i and California there's a huge swirling island of more than one trillion pieces of plastic known as the "Great Pacific Garbage Patch." An organization called The Ocean Cleanup is taking on the challenge of getting rid of the ocean's plastic trash. This successful non-profit grew out of a high-school project a kid named Boyan Slat did when he was 16! While diving in Greece, Slat came across more plastic than fish, and that experience led him to learn more about plastic pollution in oceans. Slat is now the head of the company, which has launched a full fleet of "floaters" that are capturing everything from one-ton fishing nets to microplastics! The design of the floaters is simple; it just took someone like Slat to turn an idea into a solution.

The "floater" has a long tube full of cork and buoys that rests on the surface of the sea with a screen that drops ten feet into the water. It works with the ocean currents and an anchor to create just the right speed to capture the plastic. There are several safety measures, including having people present to check for marine life before lifting the plastic out of the water.

There are 1,000 rivers responsible for 80% of the plastic that flows into the ocean, and The Ocean Cleanup has also launched 100% solar-powered floaters into those rivers. All the plastic will be brought to shore for recycling. As cities around the world place more bans on plastic bags and other throwaway items, there will be even less cleanup to do in the future.

Plastic

But what about the plastic in our landfills? Thanks to a recent innovation, there are some creepy-crawlers who might end up being our helpers! In 2017, a scientist collected larvae from wax moths in a plastic bag, only to discover later that they'd eaten the bag and gotten out. Biologists at the University of Brandon in Canada decided to study the larvae's unusual appetite and discovered that they can survive solely on polyethylene, the type of plastic used to make grocery bags. They're now studying how the larvae's gut bacteria can so easily break down the plastic, and they plan to use that knowledge to help eliminate plastic from places like landfills, where it seeps into our soil and water. Similar studies are happening at Stanford University in California, where mealworms on a diet of Styrofoam are as healthy as the ones eating wheat bran!

Consumerism

Not all important solutions come from science labs. In the last chapter, you learned how our daily value-driven choices can benefit the planet, and how many people are changing what they buy with the planet in mind. A great example is the clothes we wear, especially "fast fashion": cheap, trendy clothing that follows the latest fad, and then gets tossed out when the next fashion comes along. The tendency to want to always have new and more things is called **consumerism**. We send 13 trillion tons of clothes to landfills every year in the United States. Because they're made from so many synthetic materials, the clothes can sit in the ground for as long as 200 years before they decompose, giving off toxic chemicals and dyes that contaminate the soil and groundwater. Child labor and poor working conditions in garment factories also sound eco-justice alarms.

Environmental groups have helped raise our awareness that clothing is the second-largest polluter in the world, right after the oil industry. In response, vintage clothing stores are popping up, friends are hosting "clothing swap" parties, and people are reading labels and looking for long-lasting styles made from natural fibers. These creative options are cool for your wallet and cool for the planet.

Bouncing Back

The list of ingenious solutions to address climate change is long. Many animals, including the Arabian oryx, echo parakeet, Pinzón tortoise, lesser long-nosed bat, Louisiana black bear, Morelet crocodile, and the giant panda, have bounced back from the brink of extinction thanks to conservation work that included restoring their habitats and reducing poaching. Cities are constructing energy-efficient buildings with insulating rooftop gardens and starting to use clean-energy public transportation. Farmer's markets and community gardens are on the rise, which is a positive change from unsustainable industrial agriculture practices to local options for affordable, nutritious food. Change starts by imagining possibilities, taking on a "Let's try it!" attitude, and making it work by following through and getting support from others. Let's see what you can imagine about a future world that you'll help create.

A Pause for Feelings —
Aaahhh

You've been discovering all kinds of feelings
about climate change, and maybe now there are a
few more. How do you feel when you read about

how so many people are putting their hearts, minds, and creativity into restoring our world? Notice how you feel in your body . . . are there thoughts or images that come to your mind that match your feelings? In your journal or on a piece of paper, write about or draw these feelings.

It's Confusing!

You have been reading about well-studied changes to our world, but it can be challenging to get accurate information about climate change, especially through social media. Unfortunately, there are corporations and even charities invested in fossil fuel money that intentionally spread misinformation. For example, Germany, one of the world's largest consumers of coal, has committed to shutting down all 84 of its coal-fired power plants by 2040. That's great, and it's true! But you have to read a different article to also learn that Germany is expected to import 45 million tons of coal a year, an increase from the amount it extracted through its own plants. The United Kingdom banned fracking with the same claim of switching to renewables, but . . . the first ever shipment of shale gas from the United States was also set to arrive in Britain within 24 hours of the fracking ban being put into place.

It's always helpful to look a little deeper. Consider these guidelines:

- ◑ Where is the information coming from, and who could benefit or be harmed by it?

- ◑ If you do an internet search on the topic, what else do you learn? Is a reliable source reporting the same news?

- ◑ How do you feel when you read or hear the information? Lots of people and companies try to create a reaction like shock, anger, or joy to get people to spread information before they know the whole story. Let strong feelings be a clue that you should research the subject more.

- ◑ Does the story offer any proof?

Over time, you will learn to be a savvy media consumer and find the scientifically-based and well-researched sources you can trust.

TIME-TRAVEL

In your journal or on a piece of paper, write an entry in your diary as though it's 20 years into the future from today. The future is always unknown until we create it, and this exercise will help you envision the best possible eco-wise world for yourself and others. Have fun with it! You can either fill in the blanks in the sentences below or use the sample as an inspiration for writing about other kinds of things you want to see happen. You can also do both!

Journal Entry Date (20 years from today): _____

I'm so glad that my life_____and the world around me is _____. Climate change has _____.

Sometimes it's the little things that matter, and I really enjoy _____,
_____, and_____.

When it comes to family and work, my life is _____
_____.

I'm surprised that_____, and it makes me feel _____.

I was scared that _____ might happen, but because of _____, things turned out so differently, especially _____.

One thing I've learned about myself is _____
_____.

I've also learned that others can be
_____and_____.

I really appreciate the support I got from
_____ over the years.

I still want to learn more about _____. It makes me feel _____.

My next big project for sustaining a healthy planet is_____,

and more than anything, I really value _____
_____.

I hope that next year _____.

I'm grateful for _____.

After you've written your future journal entry, notice how you feel. Make a note to yourself to read this again at different times over the coming year in a moment when you feel discouraged: on the first day of summer break; on your birthday; and one year from today. Your "future self" journal can be like a compass that helps keep you pointed in the direction you want to go.

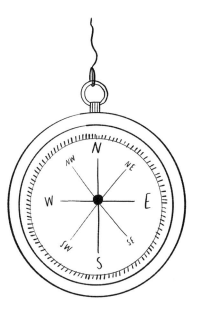

People can change some things fairly easily, but big changes usually take tremendous effort. It took activists for women's suffrage in the United States nearly 100 years to win the right to vote for women in 1920.

The Civil Rights movement was a struggle for social justice that began in the 1950s and led to successful legislation in 1964 that legally ended discrimination based on race, color, religion, and national origin—but the fight for racial justice and other equal-rights issues is far from over. The climate crisis places us in another historic period that's worthy of our greatest efforts. It's not your fault that you were born into a warming world, but it is up to all of us who live here to turn things around.

WINDOW OF TOLERANCE

As you've been learning, when we face big challenges—like becoming climate activists—we have to take even better care of our mind, body, and emotions. It's easy to have all the feelings under the sun, including anger, frustration, and sadness. But when we're overwhelmed, it doesn't just feel bad: we also can't make good decisions for ourselves, others, and the Earth. Your **window of tolerance** is where you still feel and experience the fun and challenges of life, even difficult things, without getting overwhelmed. Our window can shrink when there's a lot of stress or we aren't eating or sleeping well: We reach a point when we can't handle one more thing. But we can also learn to expand our window by practicing the things that help us cope and stay calm. All the exercises in this book are skills to help you stay within, and grow, your "window of tolerance."

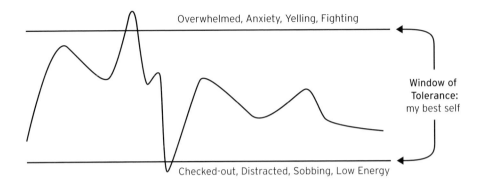

Overwhelmed, Anxiety, Yelling, Fighting

Window of Tolerance: my best self

Checked-out, Distracted, Sobbing, Low Energy

The Mindfulness Jar is another tool to help calm you down and re-enter your window of tolerance. When you're overwhelmed with strong emotions, your thoughts and feelings can swirl out of control, making it hard to think clearly. There are two parts to this next activity: Making the mindfulness jar, and then learning how to use it.

MAKING THE MINDFULNESS JAR

1. Get a clear jar with a tight-fitting lid. This could be something like a Mason jar or a clean mayonnaise or pickle jar with the labels removed.

2. Fill the jar about ¼ full with a clear school glue.

3. Then add about the same amount of fine gravel: The gravel and glue combined should fill the jar about

halfway. A good consistency for the gravel is called "fine ballast." This is available at craft stores or online where model trains and diorama materials are sold. If the rock is too fine like sand, it won't settle quickly enough. If it's too large, like aquarium pebbles, it'll settle too quickly.

4. Over the sink, fill the rest of the jar to the top with warm water and screw the lid on tightly. If the gravel falls too quickly, add more glue; if it falls to slowly, add more water.

5. If it leaks, you can get help adding silicone sealant or use a hot glue gun to seal the inner rim of the lid.

Using the Mindfulness Jar

1. When you're upset, shake the jar as hard and for as long as you want and imagine all your thoughts and feelings are like the swirling particles. Notice how they whirl around, making it very hard to see through the jar clearly.

2. When you're ready, put the jar down on a table or countertop and watch what happens when it sits still. See if you can sit as still as the jar for a few moments. Take three

slow, full breaths as you watch the gravel start to settle and the water gradually become clearer. Imagine your own thoughts and feelings drifting down to find a place to rest, just like the gravel is doing, and watch your own mind become clearer.

3. Once all the particles have landed on the bottom of the jar and the water is clear, notice how you feel. Close your eyes and take three more full breaths, giving any other thoughts or feelings that are looking for a place to rest a chance to float down and settle. When you're ready, open your eyes.

Other things can help us stay inside our window of tolerance, and those things are different for everyone: for example, sports, going for a run, talking over the problem with a friend or counselor, taking a bath, drawing, listening to music and dancing, or spending time in the park. In your journal or on a piece of paper, write down five things that help you feel relaxed, refreshed, and calm when you feel overwhelmed.

After reading this book, you now have an accurate understanding of what climate change is and why it's important. You have a deeper knowledge of your values and how they can guide your actions to help create a healthier world together. You've learned about examples of green innovations that are happening around the world. And you have a toolkit for keeping your mind and emotions clear and strong for the challenges ahead. Practice the exercises throughout the book regularly so that they're familiar and ready to use in any situation. And here's one more thing that's important to be aware of.

Not a Shame Game

Once you really feel the call to care for the Earth, it's heartbreaking to see others around you who aren't doing the same. You may have friends or family members who aren't as invested in climate action as you are, and this can stir up feelings of anger, sadness, and frustration. You might feel like lashing out when you see careless actions around you that contribute to making the climate crisis worse. But blame and shame have never been effective ways to make change. It's much more powerful to use good communication, skillful confrontation, patience, courage, empathy, endurance, support, connection, and leading by example. In the spirit of this timeless advice: "Be the change you wish to see in the world."

But you're not in this alone. Find your allies. Are there things you can do together with your family, caregivers, friends, classmates, teachers, community events, and organizations? It can be helpful to remember that you are joined by many others around the world who share the same passion and will invest their time and creativity into making a healthier world.

And (this is really important!), practice kindness and compassion towards yourself. You might be hard on yourself for not always doing everything right all the time on the planet's behalf, because now you know the urgency of the situation. The more you learn about the climate crisis, the more you'll see that there is always more that is needed. But this is a process where we learn as we go—perfection is not an option.

There may be times when you wonder whether all our eco-wise actions will be big enough and fast enough when they're competing with the machines that continue to spew carbon into the atmosphere. In those moments, it's good to remember that many important social movements have worked in the past, even when it felt impossible, and that the momentum toward healing the planet is growing every day. The Nanticoke Indian Tribe's website posted an Indigenous teaching story that reminds us of what we can do on a day-to-day, moment-by-moment basis:

> *One evening, an elderly Cherokee Brave told his grandson about a battle that goes on inside people. He said, "My son, the battle is between two 'wolves' inside us all. One is evil. It is anger, envy, jealousy, sorrow, regret, greed, arrogance, self-pity, guilt resentment, inferiority, lies, false pride, superiority, and ego. The other is good. It is joy, peace, love, hope, serenity, humility, kindness, benevolence, empathy, generosity, truth, compassion, and faith." The grandson thought about it for a minute and then asked his grandfather, "Which wolf wins?" The old Cherokee simply replied, "The one that you feed."*

Let's all work together to feed the good wolf!

ZERO HOUR AND SUNRISE

Youth have come together to create many organizations to strengthen their voices through collective action and peer support. Two of the leading youth movements are Zero Hour and Sunrise.

Zero Hour offers "training and resources for new young activists and organizers (and adults who support [their] vision) wanting to take concrete action around climate change." It was founded by Jamie Margolin, Nadia Nazar, Madelaine Tew, and Zanagee Artis. Co-founder Jamie Margolin shared that she can't recall a time when the climate crisis wasn't on her mind. She was panicking about climate change in the second grade! Jamie decided to act when she was 15, after Hurricane Maria damaged Puerto Rico and thick smoke was engulfing her hometown of Seattle from nearby wildfires, sending some of her friends with breathing problems to the hospital.

Since Zero Hour launched in 2017, they have organized youth climate marches in Washington, DC, New York, and London. They have met with lawmakers to discuss ways to reduce carbon use and ensure that people around the world have access to food, water, and housing. Climate Justice is at the heart of their efforts, and they focus on making changes where capitalism, racism, sexism, and colonialism intersect with climate issues.

Sunrise is also an American youth-led movement committed to healing the climate crisis. The members focus mainly on helping to elect government leaders who understand and support sustainability and green action. They describe their core principles as "decarbonization, jobs, and justice." The movement began with just a small grant, but in 2017 a non-profit organization was formed, and it has quickly grown to nearly 300 groups across the United States. They're now one of the most influential environmental groups in Washington, DC.

Sunrise believes that reversing climate change means reorganizing how the government operates. One project they're working on is to create "Blue-Ribbon Panels" that address the different factors that are causing climate change. The panels are made up of groups of experts who analyze a specific problem and tell the government about their ideas for solutions.

Marcela Mulholland, a Sunrise member in Florida, believes that the climate crisis is this generation's Civil Rights movement. She believes that young people have often been the ones to take positions of moral clarity in challenging times, and that they've been willing to envision and work toward what they believe the world should be. Marcela says that the current generation has a huge opportunity to model themselves on the young people who drove the Civil Rights movement, who were also fighting for crucially important social change.

How do you feel when you see how youth working together can influence important changes? What do you want to do with the opportunity you've gotten from those who came before you?

GLOSSARY

Biosphere: the worldwide combination of all eco-systems on Earth

Carbon Footprint: the amount of CO_2 and other greenhouse gasses released by a person, practice, event, etc.

Catastrophe: a terrible event; in the case of "it's a catastrophe!" a mental habit of expecting that disaster is just around the corner; our mind always imagines the worst.

Civic Engagement: working to address issues and make positive changes in a community

Climate: big patterns in the weather over a long period of time in a particular place

Climate Change: all the ways the rising temperatures are affecting plants, animals, people, and the environment

Climate Refugees: people who have been forced to leave their homes due to climate change

CO2: Carbon dioxide, the most common greenhouse gas

Colonization: movement of one people or species to a new area, where the migrant population then suppresses the native population

Consumerism: the tendency to want to always have new and more things—to "consume" goods

Desalination: removing salt from seawater in order to make it drinkable

Diversity: being made up of different elements; having a variety. In ecology, having a variety of species, habitats, etc. to make a thriving ecosystem. In society, having variety of races, cultures, genders, ages, viewpoints, etc.

DNA: deoxyribonucleic acid, the hereditary material in nearly all organisms

Drawdown: the goal of reaching a point where the level of greenhouse gases stops climbing and starts declining instead

Eco-Grief: feelings of sadness or despair caused by learning about climate change

Eco-Justice: how our environmental problems are connected to many social issues

Ecosystem: an interconnected group of living organisms

Empathy: the ability to understand and share another person's feelings

Fracking: a process used to obtain natural gas by forcing it to the surface of the Earth using heavy machinery, high pressure, and chemicals

Global Warming: the term used to describe the increasing temperature of the Earth's surface, including the oceans

Greenhouse Gas: a gas that absorbs radiation and CO_2 and thus contribute to global warming

Habitat: the natural home of an organism

Indigenous People: many different groups of First People around the world, who originally inhabited a particular place before other cultures moved in

Industrial Revolution: the period of human history when our economy shifted from largely farming and hand-made crafts to being reliant on machinery

Integrity: when your actions are consistent with your values

Jet Streams: four bands of wind and gasses high in the atmosphere that affect climate consistency

Microplastics: microscopic pieces of plastic that occur nearly everywhere in the environment because of plastic pollution

Negativity Bias: the tendency to focus on only the bad things that are happening

Overgeneralization: Coming to a big conclusion based on a little bit of evidence

Pesticides: chemicals used to kill insects

Systemic Racism: the fact that there are many policies, ideas, and actions ingrained in society that provide an unjust amount of resources to white people while denying them to people of color (also called **institutional racism**)

Weather: temporary environmental conditions like rain, sunshine, snow, or temporary temperature changes

Window of Tolerance: the emotional range in which you are your "best self"

NOTE FOR
PARENTS,
CAREGIVERS,
TEACHERS
AND
COUNSELORS

Parenting and teaching are challenging, but raising children on a planet that's heating up can feel downright daunting. We want to be guides and guardians as we teach our children about the world around them, and we also feel the natural instinct to protect them from threats and suffering. Climate change poses a dilemma: How can we help our children move forward with love, wonder, and resilience while knowing that climate change will likely impose tremendous difficulties in their future?

All the Feelings Under the Sun presents realistic and age-appropriate climate science and answers the questions that kids are asking about their changing world. It also offers effective coping tools in the form of exercises, each of which supports their curiosity and helps them build emotional resilience as their climate-change awareness grows.

It can be helpful if you read the book in its entirety as well. If you share their understanding of the material and techniques presented here, you'll be better equipped to help them with questions that might arise. Climate change is a challenging topic for most adults too, so reading the book will likely bring into focus your own complex feelings about the increasing ecological damage being done to our planet. Ideally, this is an opportunity to not only improve your parenting but also to continue your own personal growth. Seeing adults working to protect and care for the Earth by learning about and prioritizing sustainable actions carries a powerful message to kids.

Reading this book provides the opportunity to address environmental concerns as a family by engaging in eco-wise conversations and projects that everyone can participate in. An easy first step is to sit down together at home or in the classroom and brainstorm environment-focused projects that are fun or interesting: for example, create a contest to see who can avoid more single-use plastics; participate in family-friendly civic activities with a focus on sustainability; take a walk to enjoy wildflowers blooming in spring; or increase your use of green transportation by walking, taking public transportation, carpooling, and bicycling. The most important factor in helping kids cope emotionally with the reality of climate change is to empower them to become part of the solution. Helping them focus on what they can influence and control provides them with safety and reassurance—and teaches them a valuable life skill so they'll be able to think, reflect, and act effectively throughout their lives.

Kids also need a safe emotional place to express their vulnerability. They may voice fears or sadness about loss of wildlife, natural disasters, water or air pollution, the safety of friends and family, and even their pets. It's not helpful to tell them there's no reason to be upset. After validating their feelings, you can remind them that there are many people who care and are committed to making the world healthier and safer, and that they can be part of that too.

All the Feelings Under the Sun can be used alone or as a companion to therapy or classroom education. If you have a child who's prone to anxiety, it's important to be especially attentive to their responses as they read. Many of the practices offer tools for managing fears, but additional support can be very helpful. If your child is anxious and you are looking for a therapist, please see the climate-aware therapist directory on the next pages.

This book is meant to be read slowly, with plenty of time allowed for each exercise. Your child will be starting a "Making a Healthier World Together" journal to use for the practices offered in the chapters; the exercises can also be completed on sheets of paper.

As you work through the material in the book, you and your child will both be surprised at your growing resilience, which might extend beyond simply coping with a changing world: *All the Feelings Under the Sun* fosters a new frame of mind that builds creativity, empathy, a sense of belonging, and a positive shift toward making meaningful change. New relationships and connections may be forged, and you and your child can acquire tools and resources for more skillfully navigating life overall. This book is both an invitation and a map for discovering the real possibility of creating a healthier world together.

DIRECTORIES OF CLIMATE-AWARE THERAPISTS

While mental health professionals are trained to treat anxiety and depression, most clinicians do not have specific education and experience in the many social and environmental justice issues that create psychological distress related to climate change. We explore in the book how there is a broad range of feelings that are natural, and even a rational response, to our unfolding climate emergency, including overwhelm, grief, guilt: "all the feelings under the sun."

There is a newly emerging specialization in the mental health field referred to as climate-aware therapy. You may also find references to Ecopsychology, Green or Eco-Social Work, and Environmental Social Work. These professionals are much better equipped for exploring environmentally-linked feelings with an empathic and comprehensive approach.

The Climate Psychiatry Alliance and the Climate Psychology Alliance North America have created directories of mental health professionals in the United States and abroad who can deliver high-quality, climate-aware psychotherapy for climate-distressed individuals and communities. They also provide a range of educational resources, online support groups, and training.

United States: https://climatepsychology.us/

International: https://www.climatepsychology-alliance.org/support/indsupport

ACKNOWLEDGMENTS

We all owe a debt of gratitude to the young change-makers who have powerfully brought into focus the need for a book like this. I've had the opportunity to speak with many climate-aware youths taking the lead, who are curious, scared, creative, angry, and smart, and have read about many others. Special thanks to the students at Jason Lee Middle School and Stadium High in Tacoma, Washington, and their teachers Kathleen Hall and Sherry Stultz, for candid classroom conversations about climate change. It helped launch the direction for this book.

Gratitude to the American Psychological Association's kids book imprint, Magination Press, for once again having their finger on the pulse of emerging issues for kid's emotional wellbeing. Editors Katie Moore and Katie Ten Hagen provided valuable feedback to help me speak clearly to the kids they serve so well with their publications.

While writing is a solitary practice, my ideas are shaped by a lifetime of learning. Here are some of the other influencers who directly helped guide these pages:

Caroline Hickman is a leader in supporting young voices pressing for urgent change. A Climate Psychology Therapist currently teaching at the University of Bath in the UK, she generously offered her invaluable insights for bringing emotional intelligence and resilience to kids.

Nancy Dunn, president of the Fairfield-Suisun Unified Teachers Association, offered nuanced perspectives from her years of educational experience for weaving in school-based SEL (social and emotional learning) models with current science curriculum needs.

Dr. Art Blume is an Indigenous psychologist who clarified and deepened my understanding of traditional beliefs based in a profound respect for the natural world, and ways of being in harmony with all living things.

Climate Action Families is an amazing nonprofit based in Seattle that provides ways for families to work together to become more effective advocates in Climate Justice work. Their Program Director, Grace Stahre, and Climate Kids Director, Megan Slade, read the manuscript and helped prioritize the concerns voiced directly by the kids and families they see on a daily basis. It was clear wisdom from the frontlines.

My grasp of the complexities of climate science was reviewed by Heather Price, an atmospheric chemist, researcher, and Climate Justice educator. Her knowledge of climate science is simply dazzling.

Hats off once again to Madeleine Fahrenwald, wordsmith extraordinaire, who has accompanied me on many writing adventures. She possesses some kind of magic that helps my words shine.

And to the Earth, that gives us life.

About the Author

Leslie Davenport is a Marriage and Family Therapist bringing 30 years of clinical experience to the emerging field of Climate Psychology. She works as an educator and consultant to institutes recognizing the benefits of behavioral research for cultural shifts and policy change. She is the author of three previous books, including *Emotional Resiliency in the Era of Climate Change*. Leslie has worked at Ground Zero on disaster mental health teams and is on faculty with the California Institute of Integral Studies. She has offices in Tacoma, WA, and in the San Francisco Bay Area. Visit lesliedavenport.com.

About the Illustrator

Jessica Smith is a recent graduate from Falmouth University. She lives in Oxford, UK. Visit jessicasmith illustration.co.uk, @JS_Illustration on Twitter, and @Jessica_Smith_Illustration on Instagram.

About Magination Press

Magination Press is the children's book imprint of the American Psychological Association. APA works to advance psychology as a science and profession and as a means of promoting health and human welfare. Magination Press books reach young readers and their parents and caregivers to make navigating life's challenges a little easier. It's the combined power of psychology and literature that makes a Magination Press book special. Visit maginationpress.org, and @MaginationPress on Facebook, Twitter, Instagram, and Pinterest.

BIBLIOGRAPHY

Introduction

Bolton, D. (2016, January 19). *Air pollution is now a global 'public health emergency', according to the World Health Organization.* Independent. https://www.independent.co.uk/environment/air-pollution-public-health-emergency-who-world-health-organisation-a6821256.html

Davenport, L. (2017). *Emotional resiliency in the era of climate change: A clinician's guide.* Jessica Kingsley Publishers.

Fagre, D. B., McKeon, L. A., Dick, K. A., et al. (2017). Glacier margin time series (1966, 1998, 2005, 2015) of the named glaciers of Glacier National Park, MT, USA: U.S. Geological Survey. https://www.sciencebase.gov/catalog/item/58af7022e4b01ccd54f9f542?community=Northern+Rocky+Mountain+Science+Center

Gattuso, J., Magnan, A., Billé, W., et al. (2015): Contrasting futures for ocean and society from different anthropogenic CO_2 emissions scenarios. *Science, 349* (6243).

Geophysical Fluid Dynamic Laboratory: National Oceanic and Atmospheric Administration. (2020, September 23). *Global warming and hurricanes.* https://www.gfdl.noaa.gov/global-warming-and-hurricanes/

GISTEMP Team. (2020). *GISS surface temperature analysis (GISTEMP), version 4.* NASA Goddard Institute for Space Studies. https://data.giss.nasa.gov/gistemp/

Lenssen, N., Schmidt, G., Hansen, J., et al. (2019). Improvements in the GISTEMP uncertainty model. *Journal of Geophysical Research: Atmospheres, 124*(12), 6307–6326.

Lindsey, R. (2021, January 25). *Climate change: Global sea level.* National Oceanic and Atmospheric Administration. https://www.climate.gov/news-features/understanding-climate/climate-change-global-sea-level

National Centers for Environmental Information. (2018, March 23). *What's the difference between weather and climate?* https://www.ncei.noaa.gov/news/weather-vs-climate

National Oceanic and Atmospheric Administration. (2020). *Ocean acidification.* https://www.noaa.gov/education/resource-collections/ocean-coasts/ocean-acidification

Roberts, D. (2020, August 12). *Air pollution is much worse than we thought*. Vox. https://www.vox.com/energy-and-environment/2020/8/12/21361498/climate-change-air-pollution-us-india-china-deaths

Thunberg, G., Thunberg, S. (2020). *Our house is on fire: Scenes of a family and planet in crisis*. Penguin Books.

Chapter 1: How We Know What We Know

Bolano, A. (2019, March 11). *Earth timeline: From 4.5 billion years ago to today*. Science Trends. https://sciencetrends.com/earth-timeline-from-4-5-billion-years-ago-to-today/

Britannica Kids. (n.d.). *Fossil fuel*. https://kids.britannica.com/kids/article/fossil-fuel/399465#

Center for Sustainable Systems, University of Michigan. (2020). *Carbon footprint factsheet*. http://css.umich.edu/factsheets/carbon-footprint-factsheet

Chevallier, A. (2016). *Encyclopedia of herbal medicine: 550 herbs and remedies for common ailments*. DK Publishing.

Crowther, T., Glick, H., Covey, K. et al. (2015). Mapping tree density at a global scale. *Nature, 525*, 201–205.

European Parliament. (2019, March 22). *CO2 emissions from cars: Facts and figures (infographics)*. https://www.europarl.europa.eu/news/en/headlines/society/20190313STO31218/co2-emissions-from-cars-facts-and-figures-infographics

Herman, R. (1998, October 26). *How fast is the earth moving?* Scientific American. https://www.scientificamerican.com/article/how-fast-is-the-earth-mov/

Lotzof, K. (n.d.). *Are we really made of stardust?* Natural History Museum. https://www.nhm.ac.uk/discover/are-we-really-made-of-stardust.html

McCarthy, J. (2020, June 17). *This 11-year-old activist has picked up more than 100,000 pieces of plastic*. Global Citizen. https://www.globalcitizen.org/en/content/lilly-platt-activist-plastic-environment/

Mitchell, S. (2018). *Sacred instructions: Indigenous wisdom for living spirit-based change*. North Atlantic Books.

Morris, C. (2012). *The dawn of innovation: The first American industrial revolution*. PublicAffairs.

Skies & Scopes. (2020, July 3). *How many planets are there in the system, galaxy & universe?* https://skiesandscopes.com/how-many-planets/

Chapter 2: The Earth Is Heating Up

Brinkley, D. (2007). *The great deluge: Hurricane Katrina, New Orleans, and the Mississippi gulf coast*. Harper Perennial.

Climate Home News. (2015, August 14). *8-year-old takes US government to court over climate change*. https://www.climatechangenews.com/2015/08/14/8-year-old-takes-us-government-to-court-over-climate-change/

David, L., Gordon, C. (2007). *The down-to-earth guide to global warming*. Scholastic.

Goldenberg, S., Sprenger, R. (2013, May 13). *America's first climate refugees*. The Guardian. https://www.theguardian.com/environment/interactive/2013/may/13/newtok-alaska-climate-change-refugees

Hook, L. (2019, August 6). *Climate change: How the jet stream is changing your weather*. Financial Times. https://www.ft.com/content/591395fe-b761-11e9-96bd-8e884d3ea203

Joyce, C. (2018, January 12). *Scientists say a fluctuating jet stream may be causing extreme weather events*. NPR. https://www.npr.org/sections/thetwo-way/2018/01/12/577688119/scientists-say-a-fluctuating-jet-stream-may-be-causing-extreme-weather-events

Kolbert, E. (2015). *The sixth extinction: An unnatural history*. Picador.

Macy, J., Brown, M. (2014). *Coming back to life: The updated guide to the work the reconnects*. New Society Publishers.

Peach, S. (2017, August 30). *Why climate change is like a fever for the earth*. Yale Climate Connections. https://www.yaleclimateconnections.org/2017/08/why-climate-change-is-like-a-fever/

United Nations Intergovernmental Science-Policy Platform on
  Biodiversity and Ecosystem Service. (2019, May 6). *Nature's
  dangerous decline 'unprecedented': Species extension rated
  'accelerating.'* https://www.un.org/sustainabledevelopment/
  blog/2019/05/nature-decline-unprecedented-report/

Voytko, L. (2020, July 20). *Polar bears could face extinction by 2100,
  due to climate change, study says.* Forbes. https://www.forbes.
  com/sites/lisettevoytko/2020/07/20/polar-bears-could-
  face-extinction-by-2100-due-to-climate-change-study-
  says/#7c8805882276

World Health Organization. (2010). *Pakistan: The health impact of
  the floods.* https://www.who.int/hac/crises/pak/highlights/
  september2010/en/

Chapter 3: Everything is Connected

Burke, C. (2019). *Who is Indigenous teen activist Autumn Peltier?*
  Daily Dot. https://www.dailydot.com/irl/who-is-autumn-
  peltier/.

Cajete, G. (2009). *Look to the mountain: An ecology of indigenous
  education.* Kivaki Press.

Clark, A. (2019). *The poisoned city: Flint's water and the American
  urban tragedy.* Picador.

Democracy Now! (2013, February 18). *When we take care of
  the land, it takes care of us: Chief Jacqueline Thomas opposes
  Keystone XL* [video]. YouTube. https://www.youtube.com/
  watch?v=YW-aGYXK3IM

Deziel, C. (2018, July 20). *Animals that share human DNA sequences.*
  Sciencing. https://sciencing.com/animals-share-human-dna-
  sequences-8628167.html

Ignotofsky, R. (2018). *The wonderous working of planet earth:
  Understanding our world and its ecosystems.* Ten Speed
  Press.

Kerr, J., Pindar, A., Galpern, P., et al. (2015). Climate change
  impacts of bumblebees converge across continents. *Science*,
  349(6244), 177–180.

Leahy, S. (2019, April 15). *Microplastics are raining down from the sky.*
  National Geographic. https://www.nationalgeographic.com/

environment/2019/04/microplastics-pollution-falls-from-air-even-mountains/

Shubin, N. (2020). *Some assembly required: Decoding four billion years of life, from ancient fossils to DNA*. Pantheon.

Schaefer, C. (2006). *Grandmothers counsel the world*. Trumpeter.

Winter, T., Harvey, J., Franke, O., et al. (2013, January 11). *Ground water and surface water a single resource*. U.S. Department of the Interior, U.S. Geological Survey. https://pubs.usgs.gov/circ/circ1139/#pdf

Chapter 4: Practicing Eco-Justice

Craven, J., Tynes, T. (2016, February 3). *The racist roots of Flint's water crisis*. HuffPost. https://www.huffpost.com/entry/racist-roots-of-flints-water-crisis_n_56b12953e4b04f9b57d7b118

Hickel, J. (2020). *Less is more: How degrowth will save the world*. William Heinmann.

Metzger, L. (2012, March 22). *14.6 million pounds of toxic chemicals dumped into Texas' waterways*. Environment Texas. https://environmenttexas.org/news/txe/146-million-pounds-toxic-chemicals-dumped-texas%E2%80%99-waterways

Taylor, D. (2014). *Toxic communities: Environmental racism, industrial pollution, and residential mobility*. NYU Press.

Tchinda, L. (2018, June 21). *5 young environmental activists making a difference in climate change*. UN CC:Learn, Medium. https://medium.com/uncclearn/5-young-environmental-activists-making-a-difference-in-climate-change-f211e070ab53

Chapter 5: Making a Healthier World Together

Ali, M. S. (2020, July 24). *Congressman John Lewis: a champion for civil rights and environmental justice*. The Hill. https://thehill.com/opinion/energy-environment/508788-congressman-john-lewis-a-champion-for-civil-rights-and

Aziz, A. (2020, May 14). *How the Ocean Cleanup plans to work with brands to solve the problem of plastic*. Forbes. https://www.forbes.com/sites/afdhelaziz/2020/05/14/

how-the-ocean-cleanup-plans-to-work-with-brands-to-solve-the-problem-of-plastic/#66268c0d1588

Betz, B. (2020, March 4). *Scientists found a caterpillar that eats plastic. Could it help solve our plastic crisis?* Discover. https://www.discovermagazine.com/environment/scientists-found-a-caterpillar-that-eats-plastic-could-it-help-solve-our

Brown, P. (2020, February 19). *Renewable energy could power the world by 2020.* Climate News Network. https://climatenewsnetwork.net/renewable-energy-could-power-the-world-by-2050/

Burrows, S. (2020, February 28). *Tesla's solar panels are turning saltwater into drinking water for 35,000 Kenyans.* Return to Now. https://returntonow.net/2020/02/28/teslas-solar-panels-are-now-turning-saltwater-into-drinking-water-for-35000-kenyans/

Chang, S. (2020, June 14). *Seattle children's march evokes legacy of civil rights movement youth.* South Seattle Emerald. https://southseattleemerald.com/2020/06/14/seattle-childrens-march-evokes-legacy-of-civil-rights-movement-youth/

Davies, R. (2016, September 27). *First shipment of fracked shale gas set to arrive in UK.* The Guardian. https://www.theguardian.com/business/2016/sep/27/first-shipment-of-fracked-shale-gas-set-to-arrive-in-uk

DesignBoom. (2014, July 18). *Forward thinking architecture develops floating responsive agriculture.* https://www.designboom.com/architecture/forward-thinking-architecture-japa-floating-responsive-agriculture-07-18-2014/

Eckert, V. (2019, January 18). *Germany's 2019 hard coal imports seen rising after mining ends.* Reuters. https://www.reuters.com/article/us-germany-coal-vdki-idUSKCN1PC16Z

Harabbin, R. (2019, March 13). *Gas heating ban for new homes from 2025.* BBC News. https://www.bbc.com/news/science-environment-47559920

Hawken, P. (2017, March 13). *Drawdown: The most comprehensive ever proposed to reverse global warming.* Penguin Books.

Holmer, M. (2018, November 1). *Underwater meadows of seagrass could be the ideal carbon sinks.* Smithsonian Magazine. https://www.smithsonianmag.com/science-nature/

underwater-meadows-seagrass-could-be-ideal-carbon-sinks-180970686/

Horton, A., McClinton, D., Aratani, L. (2019, March 4). *Adults failed to take climate action. Meet the young activists stepping up*. The Guardian. https://www.theguardian.com/environment/2019/mar/04/can-they-save-us-meet-the-climate-kids-fighting-to-fix-the-planet

Margolies, J. (2020, February 4). 'All electric' movement picks up speed, catching some off guard. *New York Times*. https://www.nytimes.com/2020/02/04/business/all-electric-green-development.html

McCarthy, J. (2019, July 26). *Texas now gets more power from wind than coal*. Global Citizen. https://www.globalcitizen.org/en/content/texas-wind-energy-leader/

Menon, P. (2019, September 23). *New Zealand passes law aiming for net zero carbon emissions by 2050*. Reuters. https://www.reuters.com/article/us-newzealand-climate-idUSKBN1XH0RQ

Murray, R. (2019, October 3). *Jamie Margolin of zero hour is the teen climate change activist you need to know*. Today. https://www.today.com/style/jamie-margolin-zero-hour-teen-climate-change-activist-you-need-t163503

Nanticoke Indian Tribe. (n.d.). *The tale of two wolves*. https://www.nanticokeindians.org/page/tale-of-two-wolves

Phan, S. (2020, June 13). *Thousands participate in Seattle's children's march*. Komo News. https://komonews.com/news/local/thousands-participate-in-seattle-childrens-march

Possner, A., Caldeira, K. (2017, October 24). *Geophysical potential for wind energy over the open oceans*. National Academy of Sciences. https://www.pnas.org/content/114/43/11338

Ray, R. (2020, July 23). *Five things John Lewis taught us about getting in "good trouble."* Brookings. https://www.brookings.edu/blog/how-we-rise/2020/07/23/five-things-john-lewis-taught-us-about-getting-in-good-trouble/

Roth, A. (2018, October 4). *12 animals that bounced back from the brink*. National Geographic. https://www.nationalgeographic.com/animals/2018/10/animals-endangered-back-from-brink-conservation-news/

Stirpe, M. (2018, February 27). *Slowing down fast fashion with sustainability*. Northeast Recycling Council. https://nerc.org/

news-and-updates/blog/nerc-blog/2018/02/27/slowing-down-fast-fashion-with-sustainability

Temple, J. (2019, August 9). *What is geoengineering—and why should you care?* MIT Technology Review. https://www.technologyreview.com/2019/08/09/615/what-is-geoengineering-and-why-should-you-care-climate-change-harvard/

Treen, K., Williams, H., O'Neill, S. (2020, June 30). *How climate change misinformation spreads online*. Resilience. https://www.resilience.org/stories/2020-06-30/how-climate-change-misinformation-spreads-online/

Wise, J. (2019, January 27). *Germany to shut all 84 coal-fired plants to fight climate change*. The Hill. https://thehill.com/policy/energy-environment/427182-germany-to-shut-down-all-84-of-its-coal-fired-plants-to-fight